THE CROCHETER'S TREASURE CHEST

80 Classic Patterns for
Tablecloths, Bedspreads, Doilies and Edgings

EDITED BY
Mary Carolyn Waldrep

DOVER PUBLICATIONS, INC., NEW YORK

CROCHET ABBREVIATIONS

bal	balance	rnd	round
bl OR blk	block	rpt	repeat
ch	chain	sc	single crochet
dc	double crochet	s dc	short double crochet
dec	decrease	sk	skip
d tr	double treble	sl st	slip stitch
h dc	half double crochet	sp	space
inc	increase	st(s)	stitch(es)
incl	inclusive	tog	together
lp	loop	tr OR trc	treble crochet
p	picot	tr tr	triple treble (yarn
pc st	popcorn stitch		over hook 4 times)

* (asterisk) or † (dagger) . . . Repeat the instructions following the asterisk or dagger as many times as specified.

** or † † . . . Used for a second set of repeats within one set of instructions.

Repeat instructions in parentheses as many times as specified. For example. **"(Ch 5, sc in next sc) 5 times"** means to work all that is in parentheses 5 times.

Copyright © 1988 by Dover Publications, Inc.
All rights reserved under Pan American and International Copyright Conventions.

Published in Canada by General Publishing Company, Ltd., 30 Lesmill Road, Don Mills, Toronto, Ontario.

Manufactured in the United States of America
Dover Publications, Inc., 31 East 2nd Street, Mineola, N.Y. 11501

Library of Congress Cataloging in Publication Data

The Crocheter's treasure chest.

1. Crocheting—Patterns. I. Waldrep, Mary Carolyn.
TT820.C933 1988   746.43′4041   88-23702
ISBN 0-486-25833-5 (pbk.)

This Dover edition, first published in 1988, is a new selection of patterns from *Home Decoration, Book 76*, published by The Spool Cotton Company, New York, 1936; *Modern Table Settings, Book 88*, published by The Spool Cotton Company, 1937; *100 Useful Edgings, Book No. 129*, published by The Spool Cotton Company, 1939; *Bedspreads, Book No. 136*, published by The Spool Cotton Company, 1939; *Bedspreads, Book No. 151*, published by The Spool Cotton Company, 1940; *Bedspreads to Knit and Crochet, Book No. 166*, published by The Spool Cotton Company, 1941; *Edgings, Book No. 182*, published by The Spool Cotton Company, 1942; *Bedspreads to Knit and Crochet, Book No. 186*, published by The Spool Cotton Company, 1942; *Doilies, Book No. 201*, published by The Spool Cotton Company, 1943; *Bedspreads, Book No. 244*, published by The Spool Cotton Company, 1948; *Priscilla Centerpieces, Book No. 276*, published by The Spool Cotton Company, 1951; *New Ideas in Doilies, Book No. 283*, published by The Spool Cotton Company, 1952; *Edgings, Book No. 305*, published by Coats & Clark Inc., New York, 1954; *Ruffled Doilies, Book No. 306*, published by Coats & Clark Inc., 1954; *Edgings: Crocheted, Knitted, Tatted, Book 7*, published by the American Thread Company, New York, n.d.; *Star Book of Doilies, Book 22*, published by the American Thread Company, n.d.; *Conserve with Crochet . . . For the Home, Star Book No. 25*, published by the American Thread Company, n.d.; *Doilies: Crocheted and Tatted, Star Book No. 44*, published by the American Thread Company, n.d.; *Emblems and Church Laces, Star Book No. 50*, published by the American Thread Company, n.d.; *New Tablecloths, Book No. 57*, published by the American Thread Company, 1948; *Doilies, Star Doily Book No. 124*, published by the American Thread Company, 1955; *Doilies, Star Doily Book No. 151*, published by the American Thread Company, n.d.; *Crochet "County Fair," Design Book No. 51*, published by Lily Mills Company, Shelby, North Carolina, 1950; *Tablecloths for the Seasons, Crochet Design Book No. 57*, published by Lily Mills Company, n.d.; *Doilies to Treasure, Book 1600*, published by Lily Mills Company, n.d.; *Crochet for Today, Tomorrow and Always, Direction Book 1700*, published by Lily Mills Company, 1947; *Laces and Doilies, Book No. 3*, published by Royal Society, Inc., 1943; *Crisp New Doilies, Book No. 9*, published by Royal Society, Inc., 1948; *Doilies, Book No. 12*, published by Royal Society, Inc., 1951. A new Introduction has been written specially for this edition.

Table of Contents

STITCH CONVERSION CHART

U.S. Name	Equivalent
Chain	Chain
Slip	Single crochet
Single crochet	Double crochet
Half-double or short-double crochet	Half-treble crochet
Double crochet	Treble crochet
Treble crochet	Double-treble crochet
Double-treble crochet	Treble-treble crochet
Treble-treble or long-treble crochet	Quadruple-treble crochet
Afghan stitch	Tricot crochet

STEEL CROCHET HOOK CONVERSION CHART

U.S. Size	00	0	1	2	3	4	5	6	7	8	9	10	11	12	13	14
British & Canadian Size	000	00	0	1	–	1½	2	2½	–	3	–	4	–	5	–	6
Metric Size (mm)	3.00	2.75	2.50	2.25	2.10	2.00	1.90	1.80	1.65	1.50	1.40	1.25	1.10	1.00	0.75	0.60

Introduction

Crochet has long been one of the most popular forms of needlework. Instructions for crochet have been a staple of women's magazines for well over a century, and early books on the subject were eagerly sought by practitioners of the art.

During the first sixty years of the twentieth century, America's thread companies produced thousands of inexpensive instructional leaflets designed to promote their products. These leaflets featured beautiful crocheted tablecloths, bedspreads, doilies, edgings and other household items. By the 1960s, however, tastes in needlework had changed, and such crocheted accessories were no longer in favor.

Today, there is a new interest in crochet, and these now rare instruction leaflets, and the designs featured in them, have become collector's items. Here we offer directions for 80 of the finest designs from the 30s, 40s and 50s. Modern technology permits us to present them to you exactly as they originally appeared. For your convenience, we have arranged the designs into four categories—Tablecloths and Placemats, Bedspreads, Doilies and Edgings.

A number of the threads called for in the directions are still available; if not, other, similar threads can easily be found. Be careful when buying threads, however, because some product names used in the past are now being reused on completely different threads. If using colored threads, be sure to buy enough at one time to complete your project, since dye lots can vary considerably.

Many of the patterns in the book list a gauge—the number of stitches per inch or the size of the individual motifs or blocks. However, not all patterns give this information. Doilies often list only a finished size, while a few patterns do not even do this. In these cases, a small variation in the size of the design will make little difference to the appearance of the finished piece. Whether there is a gauge listed or not, the number of stitches and rows should be the same as indicated in the directions. Work a sample of the pattern using the suggested thread and hook and compare it to the gauge if one is listed. If

your piece is too big, use a smaller hook; if too small, use a larger hook. If no gauge is stated, check the appearance of your work—if the stitches are loose and untidy, use a smaller hook; if they are crowded, use a larger hook. Edgings are a special case and can be made using a variety of threads, depending on the desired effect. Just remember, the finer the thread, the smaller the hook required.

Your finished piece will be improved by careful washing and blocking. For large projects that are made up of many units sewn together, you may find it easier to block the individual pieces before joining them. Use a neutral soap and cool water. Gently squeeze the suds through the crochet; do not rub. Rinse thoroughly. Pad a flat surface with several layers of thick terry toweling. Using rustproof pins, pin the piece, right side down, on the surface, pinning each picot and loop in place. When the crochet is almost dry, press it through a damp cloth with a moderately hot iron. Do not allow the iron to rest on the stitches, particularly the raised stitches.

To give a crisper look to doilies, starch them after washing. Mix the starch solution following the manufacturer's directions and immerse the piece in the solution, squeezing it through the stitches. Squeeze out the excess and pin the piece in place as described above. For a ruffled doily, use a very heavy starch solution and pin the piece *right side up*, leaving the ruffle free. Shape the ruffle with your fingers as the piece dries.

The terminology and hooks listed in this book are those used in the United States. The charts opposite give the U.S. names of crochet stitches and their equivalents in other countries and the approximate equivalents to U.S. crochet hook sizes. Crocheters should become thoroughly familiar with the differences in both crochet terms and hook sizes before starting any project.

The stitches used in the projects in this book are explained on page 95. A metric conversion chart is located on page 96.

Tableclothes and Placemats

Mayfair Dinner Set

Materials: Clark's O.N.T. Mercerized Crochet, Size 50, White, 13 balls; or J. & P. Coats 8 balls. 1-1/3 yards of 36 or 39 inch pastel linen. Milward's steel crochet hook No. 11.

Fan Medallion measures about 4½ inches on each straight edge.

Fan Medallion: * Ch 5, d c in 1st st of ch, working off only 2 loops, d c in same st, working off only 2 loops, thread over and draw through remaining loops on hook. Repeat from * making 40 scallops. Break thread but do not fasten off. **2nd row:** Attach thread between 18th and 19th scallops, counting from start of row, ch 8, tr tr between 2nd and 3rd scallops to left, ch 8, s c between next 2nd and 3rd scallops to left. Fasten off. **3rd row:** Attach thread between next 3rd and 4th scallops from start of last row. * Ch 6, Clones knot in 4th ch from hook. (To make Clones knot, thread over, insert hook in 4th ch from hook and draw up a loop, bring it forward and up and thread over again as for a d c. Continue to draw up loops from over and under the ch for 8 times (16 loops over hook). Draw thread through all loops on hook at once, thread over and draw through loop on hook, and make an s c around ch at base of knot,

drawing tight which completes the knot.) Then ch 2, skip 2 sts of ch of last row, make long tr tr (thread over 5 times) in next st. Repeat from * 4 more times. Ch 6, knot, ch 2, s c between 3rd and 4th scallops. Fasten off. **4th row:** Attach thread between next 3rd and 4th scallops from start of last row. * Ch 7, knot, ch 3, long tr tr over long tr tr of row below. Repeat from * 4 more times. Ch 7, knot, ch 3, s c between 3rd and 4th scallops. Fasten off. **5th, 6th, 7th rows:** Continue working same way, with longer chs between knots. For 5th row, ch 8, knot, ch 4; 6th row, ch 9, knot, ch 5; 7th row, ch 11, knot, ch 7. **8th row:** Attach thread close to last scallop made, * long tr tr over next long tr tr of previous row, 5 scallops (same as for 1st row), repeat 5 more times, joining last scallop with sl st to 1st scallop of 1st row. **9th row:** Ch 11, d c in 1st st of ch, * ch 4, d c between next 2 scallops. Repeat from * along both sides of fan, making ch 7, d c in same st at point. Around curve of fan, ch 5, d c between next 2 scallops, joining last ch 5 to 3rd st of 1st ch 11. Fasten off.

Make 4 fan medallions for each plate doily and center runner. Pin medallions into shape and press with a

Continued on page 13

9

Poinsettia Tablecloth

Materials Required—

AMERICAN THREAD COMPANY
"STAR" MERCERIZED CROCHET COTTON.
ARTICLE 20. SIZE 20

38—250 yd. Balls Cream, Ecru or White or "Gem" Mercerized Crochet Cotton, Article 35, Size 20.
32—300 yd. Balls.
Steel Crochet Hook #11.

Each motif measures about 4¼ inches. 221 motifs 13x17 are required for cloth measuring about 55x72 inches without edge.

MOTIF—Ch 8, join to form a ring, ch 1 and work 16 s c in ring, join in 1st s c.

2nd Row—Ch 7, sl st in 5th st from hook for picot, ch 2, skip 1 s c, s c in next s c, repeat from beginning all around.

3rd Row—Sl st to center of picot, * ch 8, s c in next picot, repeat from * 6 times, ch 4, d c in 1st picot (this brings thread in position for next row).

4th Row—Ch 4, 4 d c over same loop, work 4 d c, ch 1, 4 d c over each remaining loop working 3 d c over remainder of 1st loop, join in 3rd st of ch.

5th Row—Sl st in next st of ch, * ch 7, 7 tr c with ch 1 between each tr c in next ch 1 loop, ch 7, s c in next ch 1 loop, repeat from * 3 times.

6th Row—Sl st to center of loop, s c over same loop, ** ch 5, s c in next ch 1 loop, * ch 3, s c in next ch 1 loop, repeat from * 4 times, ch 5, s c in next loop, ch 6, s c in next loop, repeat from ** twice, ch 5, s c in next ch 1 loop, * ch 3, s c in next ch 1 loop, repeat from * 4 times, ch 5, s c in next loop, ch 2, d c in 1st s c.

7th Row—Ch 3, 2 d c over same loop, ** ch 3, s c in next loop, ch 5, s c in next loop, * ch 3, s c in next loop, repeat from * 3 times, ch 5, s c in next loop, ch 3, 3 d c in next loop, repeat from ** twice, ch 3, s c in next loop, ch 5, s c in next loop, * ch 3, s c in next loop, repeat from * 3 times, ch 5, s c in next loop, ch 3, join in 3rd st of ch.

8th Row—Ch 4, 2 tr c in same space, ** ch 7, skip 1 d c, 3 tr c in next d c, ch 3, skip next 3 ch loop, s c in next 5 ch loop, ch 5, s c in next loop, * ch 3, s c in next loop, repeat from * twice, ch 5, s c in next loop, ch 3, 3 tr c in next d c, repeat from ** twice, ch 7, skip 1 d c, 3 tr c in next d c, ch 3, skip next 3 ch loop, s c in next 5 ch loop, ch 5, s c in next loop, * ch 3, s c in next loop, repeat from * twice, ch 5, s c in next loop, ch 3, join in 4th st of ch.

9th Row—Ch 4, 1 tr c in each of the next 2 tr c, ** ch 7, s c in next loop, ch 7, 1 tr c in each of the next 3 tr c, ch 3, skip next 3 ch loop, s c in next 5 ch loop, ch 5, s c in next loop, * ch 3, s c in next loop, repeat from * once, ch 5, s c in next loop, ch 3, 1 tr c in each of the next 3 tr c, repeat from ** twice, ch 7, s c in next loop, ch 7, 1 tr c in each of the next 3 tr c, ch 3, skip next 3 ch loop, s c in next 5 ch loop, ch 5, s c in next loop, * ch 3, s c in next loop, repeat from * once, ch 5, s c in next loop, ch 3, join in 4th st of ch.

10th Row—Ch 4, 1 tr c in each of the next 2 tr c, * ch 9, s c in next loop, ch 9, s c in next loop, ch 9, 1 tr c in each of the next 3 tr c, ch 3, skip next 3 ch loop, s c in next 5 ch loop, ch 5, s c in next loop, ch 3, s c in next loop, ch 5, s c in next loop, ch 3, 1 tr c in each of the next 3 tr c, repeat from * twice, ch 9, s c in next loop, ch 9, s c in next loop, ch 9, 1 tr c in each of the next 3 tr c, ch 3, skip

next 3 ch loop, s c in next 5 ch loop, ch 5, s c in next loop, ch 3, s c in next loop, ch 5, s c in next loop, ch 3, join in 4th st of ch.

11th Row—Ch 4, 1 tr c in each of the next 2 tr c, ** ch 9, s c in next loop, ch 5, work 4 cluster sts with ch 5 between each cluster st in next loop (cluster st: * thread over twice, insert in loop, pull through and work off 2 loops, twice, repeat from * twice, thread over and work off all loops at one time), ch 5, s c in next loop, ch 9, 1 tr c in each of the next 3 tr c, ch 3, skip next 3 ch loop, s c in next 5 ch loop, * ch 5, s c in next loop, repeat from * once, ch 3, 1 tr c in each of the next 3 tr c, repeat from ** twice, ch 9, s c in next loop, ch 5, work 4 cluster sts with ch 5 between each cluster st in next loop, ch 5, s c in next loop, ch 9, 1 tr c in each of the next 3 tr c, ch 3, skip next 3 ch loop, s c in next 5 ch loop, * ch 5, s c in next loop, repeat from * once, ch 3, join in 4th st of ch.

12th Row—Ch 4, 1 tr c in each of the next 2 tr c, ** ch 9, s c in next loop, * ch 5, cluster st in next loop, repeat from * 4 times, ch 5, s c in next loop, ch 9, 1 tr c in each of the next 3 tr c, ch 3, skip next 3 ch loop, 1 s c in each of the next 2 loops, ch 3, 1 tr c in each of the next 3 tr c, repeat from ** twice, ch 9, s c in next loop, * ch 5, cluster st in next loop, repeat from * 4 times, ch 5, s c in next loop, ch 9, 1 tr c in each of the next 3 tr c, ch 3, skip next 3 ch loop, 1 s c in each of the next 2 loops, ch 3, join in 4th st of ch.

Continued on page 13

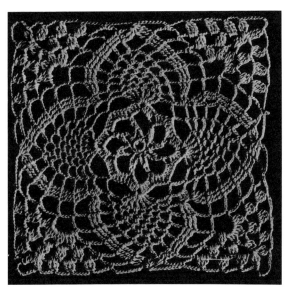

Sundial Tray Mat

Materials: Choose one of the following threads in White or Ecru:

Clark's O.N.T. Mercerized Crochet, size 10, 6 balls.
J. & P. Coats Mercerized Crochet, size 10, 6 balls.
J. & P. Coats Big Ball, size 10, 3 balls.
Clark's Big Ball, size 10, 3 balls.
Milward's steel crochet hook No. 6.

Large motif measures about 4¾ inches. When completed, mat measures about 14 × 19 inches.

Large Motif. To begin, ch 10, join with sl st to form ring. **1st rnd:** Ch 3, 23 d c in ring. Join with sl st to 3rd ch of ch-3 first made. **2nd rnd:** Ch 3, d c in each of next 2 d c, ch 2, * d c in each of next 3 d c, ch 2. Repeat from * around. Join with sl st to 3rd ch of ch-3 first made. **3rd rnd:** Ch 3, d c in st from which ch-3 was started, d c in next d c, 2 d c in last d c, ch 2, * 2 d c in 1st d c of next group of d c, d c in next d c, 2 d c in last d c of group, ch 2, repeat from * around. Join with sl st. **4th rnd:** Ch 3, d c in st from which ch-3 was started, d c in each of next 3 d c, 2 d c in last d c, ch 2, * 2 d c in 1st d c of next group of d c, d c in each of next 3 d c, 2 d c in last d c of group, ch 2. Repeat from * around. Join with sl st. **5th rnd:** Ch 3, d c in st from which ch-3 was started, d c in each of next 5 d c, 2 d c in last d c, ch 3, * 2 d c in 1st d c of next group of d c, d c in each of next 5 d c, 2 d c in last d c of group, ch 3, repeat from * around. Join with sl st. **6th rnd:** Ch 3, d c in st from which ch-3 was started, d c in each of next 3 d c, ch 3, skip next d c, d c in each of next 3 d c, 2 d c in last d c, ch 3, * 2 d c in 1st d c of next group of d c, d c in each of next 3 d c, ch 3, skip next d c, d c in each of next 3 d c, 2 d c in last d c, ch 3. Repeat from * around. Join with sl st. **7th rnd:** Sl st in each d c to next ch-3, ch 6, d c in same ch-3 sp, ch 3, d c in same sp, ch 3, d c in same sp, ch 4, s c in next ch-3 sp, ch 4, * d c in next ch-3 sp, ch 3, d c in same sp, ch 3, d c in same sp, ch 3, d c in same sp, ch 4, s c in next ch-3 sp, ch 4. Repeat from * around. Join with sl st in 3rd ch of ch-6 first made. **8th rnd:** Ch 8, tr in next sp, ch 2, tr in next ch-3 sp, ch 2, tr in same sp, ch 2, tr in next ch-3 sp, ch 2, tr in same sp, ch 4, s c in next s c, ch 4, * tr in next ch-3 sp, ch 2, tr in same sp, ch 2, tr in next ch-3 sp, ch 2, tr in same sp, ch 2, tr in next ch-3 sp, ch 2, tr in same sp, ch 4, s c in next s c, ch 4, repeat from * around. Join with sl st in 6th ch of ch-8 first made. **9th rnd:** Ch 5, s c in next ch-2 sp, * ch 5, s c in next ch-2 sp, ch 5, s c in next ch-2 sp, ch 5, s c in next ch-2 sp, ch 5, s c in next ch-2 sp, ch 6, s c in next ch-2 sp, ch 5, s c in same ch-2 sp. Repeat from * around. Join with sl st in 1st ch of ch-5 first made. **10th rnd:** Ch 5, s c in next ch-5 loop, * ch 5, s c in next ch-5 loop, ch 5, s c in next ch-5 loop, ch 5, s c in next ch-5 loop, ch 5, s c in next ch-5 loop, ch 2, s c in ch-6 loop, ch 2, s c in next ch-5 loop, ch 5, s c in same ch-2 sp. Repeat from * around. Join with sl st. Break off.
Make 12 of these large motifs.

Small Motif. To begin, ch 10, join. **1st and 2nd rnds:** Same as 1st and 2nd rnds of Large Motif. **3rd rnd:** * Ch 5, s c in 2nd d c of 3-dc group, ch 5, s c in next ch-2 sp. Repeat from * 7 more times. **4th rnd:** * Ch 5, s c in next sp. Repeat from * 16 more times. Break off.
Make 6 of these small motifs.

Joining Motifs. Place motifs in position with the small motifs to fill in spaces left open by large motifs. With a sewing needle and crochet cotton, sew motifs together with 2 or 3 over and over stitches. Do not break off thread, but make a running stitch through the ch-loop on one motif to as far as center of next ch-loop. Be careful not to draw thread too tight. Take 2 or 3 over and over stitches in the center of this loop and the one on the other motif to join the 2 motifs together. Thus continue joining around blocks.

Mayfair Dinner Set

Continued from page 9

damp cloth. Cut colored linen 12 by 18 inches for plate doilies and 12 by 30 inches for runner. Sew a fan medallion in place in each corner, making allowance that after linen is hemmed between medallions, the beading row of ch 5 and d c around curve of fan will extend out beyond edge of hemmed linen. Cut out corners of linen allowing ⅛ inch to turn back. Slash at inside corners. Work over edge of medallion and linen closely with Six Strand Floss, using 2 strands doubled. Then hem edges of linen between medallions and work a beading row across linen edges, joining the beading rows around curve of fans. Make beading rows ch 4, d c. When complete, work around doily with 4 s c over each ch and s c over s c. **Edge.** Ch 4, 2 d c in top of last s c, working off only 2 loops of each d c, thread over and draw thread through remaining loops, * ch 11, knot, ch 7, 3 d c in 10th s c on edge, working off d c's as before. Repeat from * around.

Circular Medallion for Runner. Make a row of 40 scallops as for 1st row of fan. Fasten off. Make another row of 20 scallops, sl st between 20th and 21st scallops of 1st row, then make 20 more scallops. Fasten off. Attach thread between 2nd and 3rd scallop of 1 row, counting from center crossing, * ch 8, d tr in center crossing, ch 8, 1 sl st between 2nd and 3rd scallops of next row. Repeat from * around and join with sl st to start of row and fasten off. **3rd row:** Attach thread between next 3rd and 4th scallops and make same as 3rd row of fan, crossing over each of the 4 rows of scallops working around complete circle. **4th to 7th rows incl:** Same as corresponding rows of fan. **8th row:** Attach thread to end of 1 row of scallops, make * 5 scallops, long tr tr over next long tr tr of previous row and repeat from * 5 more times, joining to end of next row of scallops with 1 s c. Continue around. **9th row:** Ch 9, 1 d c between next 2 scallops, * ch 5, 1 d c between next 2 scallops and repeat from * around. Fasten off. Set circular medallion into linen runner and finish with an edging the same as for the fan medallions.

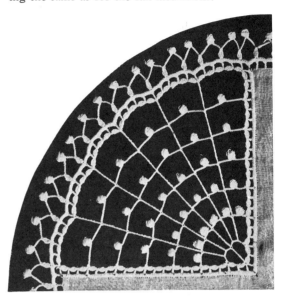

Poinsettia Tablecloth

Continued from page 11

13th Row—Sl st across each tr c and to center st of next loop, s c over same loop, * ch 5, cluster st in next loop, repeat from * twice, ch 5, cluster st in next cluster st, ch 11, cluster st in same space, * ch 5, cluster st in next loop, repeat from * twice, ch 5, s c in next loop, ch 9, * thread over twice, insert in next tr c and work off 2 loops twice, repeat from * 5 times, thread over and work off all loops at one time, ch 9, s c in next loop, continue all around in same manner ending row with ch 9, sl st in 1st s c, break thread.

Work a 2nd motif in same manner joining to 1st motif in last row as follows: sl st to center of 1st loop, s c in same loop, * ch 5, cluster st in next loop, repeat from * twice, ch 5, cluster st in next cluster st, ch 6, sl st in corresponding loop of 1st motif, ch 6, cluster st in same cluster st of 2nd motif, * ch 3, sl st in corresponding loop of 1st motif, ch 3, cluster st in next loop of 2nd motif, repeat from * twice, ch 3, sl st in corresponding loop of 1st motif, ch 3, s c in next loop of 2nd motif, ch 5, sl st in corresponding loop of 1st motif, ch 5, * thread over twice, insert in next tr c of 2nd motif, pull through and work off 2 loops twice, repeat from * 5 times, thread over and work off all loops at one time, ch 5, sl st in corresponding loop of 1st motif, ch 5, s c in next loop of 2nd motif, * ch 3, sl st in corresponding loop of 1st motif, ch 3, cluster st in next loop of 2nd motif, repeat from * twice, ch 3, sl st in corresponding loop of 1st motif, ch 3, cluster st in next cluster st of 2nd motif, ch 6, sl st in corresponding loop of 1st motif, ch 6, cluster st in same cluster st of 2nd motif and complete motif same as 1st motif.

Join 3rd motif to 2nd motif and 4th motif to 3rd and 1st motifs in same manner.

EDGE: Attach thread at joining at right hand side before corner, ch 4, cluster st in same space, ch 4, sl st in top of cluster st for picot, ch 5, s c in next loop, ch 4, sl st in top of s c for picot, * ch 5, cluster st in next loop, ch 4, sl st in top of cluster st for picot, ch 5, s c in next loop, ch 4, sl st in top of s c for picot, repeat from * once, ch 5, cluster st in next loop, picot, ch 5, s c in top of tr c group, ch 4, sl st in top of s c for picot, * ch 5, cluster st in next loop, picot, ch 5, s c in next loop, picot, repeat from * twice, ch 5, cluster st in same space, picot, ch 6, sl st in 4th st from hook for picot, ch 2, cluster st in same space, picot, ch 5, s c in same space, picot, (corner) * ch 5, cluster st in next loop, picot, ch 5, s c in next loop, picot, repeat from * once, ch 5, cluster st in next loop, picot, ch 5, s c in top of tr c group, picot, * ch 5, cluster st in next loop, picot, ch 5, s c in next loop, picot, repeat from * twice, ** ch 5, cluster st in joining, picot, * ch 5, s c in next loop, picot, ch 5, cluster st in next loop, picot, repeat from * twice, ch 5, s c in top of tr c group, picot, * ch 5, cluster st in next loop, picot, ch 5, s c in next loop, picot, repeat from * twice, repeat from ** all around working all corner motifs same as 1st corner motif.

If napkins are desired, cut linen the required size. Roll a narrow hem and work a row of s c over hem. Finish with edge same as on cloth.

Pond Lily Tablecloth

Materials Required—

AMERICAN THREAD COMPANY

"STAR" MERCERIZED CROCHET COTTON.

ARTICLE 20. SIZE 20

36—250 yd. Balls Cream, Ecru or White or "Gem" Mercerized Crochet Cotton, Article 35, Size 20.
30—300 yd. Balls.
Steel Crochet Hook #11.

Each motif measures about 4½ inches. 192 Motifs 12x16 are required for cloth measuring about 56x74 inches with edge.

MOTIF—Ch 8, join to form a ring, ch 3 and work 23 d c into ring, join in 3rd st of ch.

2nd Row—Ch 12, sl st in 7th st from hook, ch 5, skip 2 d c, s c in next d c, repeat from beginning all around.

3rd Row—5 s c over next loop, sl st in next loop, ch 4, * thread over twice, insert in same loop, pull through and work off 2 loops twice, repeat from * once, thread over and work off all loops at one time, ** ch 5, * thread over twice, insert in same loop, pull through and work off 2 loops twice, repeat from * twice, thread over and work off all loops at one time, repeat from ** twice, ch 5, * thread over twice, insert in same loop, pull through and work off 2 loops twice, repeat from * once, thread over and work off all loops at one time, ch 4, sl st in same loop, 5 s c in next loop, repeat from beginning all around.

4th Row—Sl st across next 5 s c, the ch 4 and to the center of next loop, s c in same loop, * ch 6, s c in next loop, repeat from * twice, s c in next loop, repeat from 1st * all around, join in 1st s c.

5th Row—Sl st in each of the next 2 chs, 3 s c in same loop, * ch 6, 3 s c in next loop, repeat from * all around ending row with ch 3, d c in 1st s c (this brings thread in position for next row).

6th Row—Ch 4 (ch 4 at beginning of row counts as 1 tr c), 2 tr c in same space, * ch 5, 3 s c in next loop, repeat from * once, ch 5, then repeat from beginning all around, join in 4th st of ch.

7th Row—Ch 4, 2 tr c in same space, * ch 7, skip next tr c, 3 tr c in next tr c, ch 6, skip next loop, 5 s c in next loop, ch 6, 3 tr c in next tr c, repeat from * all around, ending row with ch 7, skip next tr c, 3 tr c in next tr c, ch 6, skip next loop, 5 s c in next loop, ch 6, join in 4th st of ch.

8th Row—Ch 4, 1 tr c in each of the next 2 tr c, * ch 7, 3 s c in next loop, ch 7, 1 tr c in each of the next 3 tr c, ch 6, skip 1 s c, 1 s c in each of the next 3 s c, ch 6, 1 tr c in each of the next 3 tr c, repeat from * all around ending row with ch 7, 3 s c in next loop, ch 7, 1 tr c in each of the next 3 tr c, ch 6, skip 1 s c, 1 s c in each of the next 3 s c, ch 6, join in 4th st of ch.

9th Row—Ch 4, 1 tr c in each of the next 2 tr c, * ch 7, 3 s c in next loop, ch 7, 3 s c in next loop, ch 7, 1 tr c in each of the next 3 tr c, ch 6, s c in center s c of s c group, ch 6, 1 tr c in each of the next 3 tr c, repeat from * all around in same manner, join in 4th st of ch.

10th Row—Ch 4 (counts as 1 tr c), 1 tr c in each of the next 2 tr c, * ch 7, 3 s c in next loop, repeat from * twice, ch 7, 1 tr c in each of the next 3 tr c, repeat from beginning all around, join, break thread.

Work a 2nd motif in same manner joining to 1st motif in last row as follows: ch 4, 1 tr c in each of the next 2 tr c, * ch 7, 3 s c in next loop, repeat from * once, ch 3, sl st in corresponding loop of 1st motif, ch 3, 3 s c in next loop of 2nd motif, ch 3, sl st in next loop of 1st motif, ch 3, 1 tr c in each of the next 6 tr c of 2nd motif, * ch 3, sl st in corresponding loop of 1st motif, ch 3, 3 s c in next loop of 2nd motif, repeat from * once and complete motif same as 1st motif, break thread.

Join 3rd motif to 2nd motif and 4th motif to 3rd and 1st motifs in same manner.

JOINING MOTIF—Ch 8, join to form a ring, ** ch 4, * thread over twice, insert in ring, pull through and work off 2 loops twice, repeat from *, thread over and work off all loops at one time, ch 4, 3 s c in ring, repeat from ** 3 times.

2nd Row—Sl st to top of ch 4, ch 3, 2 d c in same space, * ch 6, skip next st, 3 d c in next st, ch 5, 3 d c in top of next ch 4, repeat from * twice, ch 6, skip next st, 3 d c in next st, ch 5, join in 3rd st of ch.

3rd Row—Ch 3 (ch 3 at beginning of row counts as 1 d c), 1 d c in each of the next 2 d c, ch 6, 3 s c in next loop, ch 6, 1 d c in each of the next 3 d c, ch 3, s c in next loop, ch 3, repeat from beginning all around, join in 3rd st of ch.

4th Row—Ch 4, 1 tr c in each of the next 2 d c, ch 3, sl st in 3rd free loop of any large motif, ch 3, 3 s c in next loop of joining motif, ch 3, sl st in next free loop of same large motif, ch 3, sl st in next free loop of next large motif, ch 3, 3 s c in next loop of joining motif, ch 3, sl st in next loop of same large motif, ch 3, tr c in each of the next 6 d c of joining motif and continue in same manner until joining is completed.

Continued on page 17

Empire Medallion Tea Cloth

Materials: Choose one of the following threads in White or Ecru:

    Clark's O.N.T. Mercerized Crochet, size 30, 15 balls.

    J. & P. Coats Mercerized Crochet, size 30, 12 balls.

    J. & P. Coats Big Ball, size 30, 6 balls.

    Milward's steel crochet hook No. 10, and 1⅓ yards linen, 36 inches wide, for cloth about 50 inches square.

Medallion measures about 6 inches square.

Medallions: Ch 7, join with sl st to form ring. **1st rnd:** 12 s c in ring. Join with sl st to s c first made. **2nd rnd:** Ch 6, * d c in next s c, ch 3, repeat from * around, join with sl st to 3rd st of ch-6 (12 d c counting ch). **3rd rnd:** * Over next ch loop, 1 half d c, 3 d c, 1 half d c, repeat from * around. **4th rnd:** Ch 9, d c between next 2 scallops, * ch 6, d c between next 2 scallops and repeat from * around, ch 6, join with sl st to 3rd st of ch-9. **5th rnd:** Ch 3, * 6 d c over next ch, d c over d c, repeat from * around, join with sl st to 3rd st of ch-3. Sl st over next d c. **6th rnd:** Ch 3, d c in each of next 5 d c, * ch 5, 1 s c in 1st st to make p, ch 1, skip next d c. D c in each of next 6 d c and repeat from * around, joining last ch-1 with sl st to 3rd st of ch-3. **7th rnd:** Ch 3, d c over

d c then ch 1, ch-5 p, ch 2 and d c over d c as in previous rnd.

8th, 9th and 10th rnds: Same as 7th except for p loops between. (8th) Ch 2, ch-5 p, ch 3. (9th) Ch 3, ch-5 p, ch 4. (10th) Ch 4, ch-5 p, ch 5. **11th rnd:** Ch 3, * d c in next st, d c in next, but work off only 2 loops, then d c in next and work off 2 loops, thread over and draw through the 3 loops remaining on hook, d c in each of next 2 sts, ch 11, d c in next d c and repeat from * around, joining last ch-11 to 3rd st of ch-3. **12th rnd:** * Ch 3, d c in each of next 3 sts, working off only 2 loops of each, thread over and draw through 2 loops, thread over and draw through remaining loops on hook. Make a 5 ch p in top of d c, ch 4, sl st in next st, ch 1. Over ch 11 make 8 s c, a ch-5 p, 8 s c over remainder of ch, 1 sl st in 1st st of next group. Repeat from * around. Sl st to tip of 1st point.

13th rnd: Ch 8, * a ch-5 p, ch 5, tr in next p, ch 5, repeat from * around, ch 5, and join to 4th st of ch-8. * Ch 8, make a ch-5 p, ch 3, d tr in next tr, ch 3, a ch-5 p, ch 3, d tr in same st, ch 3, a ch-5 p, ch 8, s c in next tr. Fasten off. Skip 3 tr, join to next tr, and repeat from * 3 more times, to form the 4 corners.

Heading rnd: Join to the p of 1 corner loop, ch 15, d tr in next d tr, ** ch 8, skip next p, tr in 4th st of ch beyond, ch 8, skip next p loop, tr in next tr, * ch 8, tr in next tr, repeat from * once, ch 8, skip next p, 1 tr in 4th st of next ch, ch 8, 1 d tr in next d tr, ch 8, 1 d tr in next corner p, ch 8, 1 d tr in next d tr. Repeat from ** around, fastening ch-8 at end of row to 8th st of ch-15.

Beading rnd: Ch 8, d c in same st, * ch 2, skip next 2 sts, d c in next and repeat from * around, making 1 d c, ch 5, 1 d c in same st in each corner. End rnd with sl st in 3rd st of 1st ch 8. Make 24 more medallions. Stretch and pin in perfect squares and press with a damp cloth.

Cut squares of linen slightly larger than medallions (to allow for hem), and hem to measure the same as the beading row along one edge of medallion.

On 12 of the linen squares sew a beading row on one side. To make beading, ch 125, d c in 8th ch from hook, * ch 2, skip 2 sts, d c in next, and repeat from * along ch. Whip medallions to linen squares in checkerboard style, using the 12 squares with beading for the outside edge. For the first row use 4 medallions and 3 linen squares, so that the completed cloth has a medallion in each corner.

Edge: Make a solid row of d c around, with 2 d c over each ch 2 and d c over d c, and 5 d c in each corner. **2nd row:** Starting at 1 corner, ch 11, * a ch-5 p, ch 6, skip 13 sts, d tr in next, ch 6, and repeat from * around. At each corner d c make 1 d tr, ch 13 and 1 d tr. End row with sl st in 4th st of 1st loop. **3rd, 4th and 5th rows:** Make the same p loops as in 2nd row, making the d tr's over the d tr's of previous row. At each corner make a d tr in d tr, ch 6, d tr in center st of ch-13, ch 13, d tr in same st, ch 6 and continue around. **6th row:** Ch 21, d tr in next d tr, ch 13, d tr in next d tr around. At each corner make 1 d tr, ch 13, 1 d tr in same st and 1 extra ch 6 before and after corner sts. Finish row with sl st in 9th st of 1st loop. **7th row:** 13 s c over each ch-13 loop and 6 s c over each ch-6 loop. Fasten off. **8th row:** Join to 5th s c of a 13-s c loop, ch 3, 1 d c in each of next 4 s c, * ch 2, a ch-5 p, ch 4, skip 4 s c of next loop, d c in each of next 5 s c, and repeat from * around. At corner loops, skip 4 s c, 1 d c in each of next 5 s c, ch 2, a ch-5 p, ch 3, skip 4 s c, 1 d c in each of next 5 s c. Finish row with sl st in ch 3 at start of row. **9th row:** Ch 3, 1 d c in next d c, 1 d c in each of next 2 d c, working off only 2 loops of each, thread over and draw through remaining loops of hook, d c in next d c, ch 10, 5 d c in next group (working off the 3rd and 4th together), repeat

around. At corners make ch 15 between groups of d c. End row with sl st in ch 3 at start of row.

10th row: * Ch 3, d c in each of next 2 d c, working off only 2 loops of each, thread over and draw through all loops on hook. A ch-5 p, ch 3, sl st in next d c, ch 1, 5 s c, a ch 5 p, 5 s c over next ch 10, sl st in 1st d c of next group. Repeat from * around Break thread and fasten off.

Napkins: Join to a corner of hemmed edge, ch 8, 1 d c in same place, ch 2, 1 d c in edge about ⅛ inch away. Repeat around. Make 2 d c with ch 5 between at each corner. End row with sl st in 3rd st of 1st ch 8. **2nd row:** Make a solid row of d c around, making 2 d c over each ch 2 and d c in each d c, with 5 d c in the 3rd st of each ch 5 at corners. Fasten off. **3rd row:** Join to 1 corner, ch 29, 1 d tr in same place, ch 14, 1 d tr in about 14th or 15th d c along edge. Repeat around, adjusting spacing of d tr so that ch 14's are stretched nearly straight and taut. At each corner make ch 20 between d tr. End row with sl st in 9th st of 1st loop. **4th row:** 14 s c over each ch 14, and 25 s c over each corner loop. Fasten off. **5th row:** Follow directions for 8th row of edge on cloth, except that in corner loops, leave 3 s c between 2 groups of d c. Complete by following directions for 9th and 10th rows of the edging for the cloth

Pond Lily Tablecloth

Continued from page 15

EDGE: Attach thread in 3rd loop on right hand side before joining of corner motif, ch 1 and work 3 s c in same space, ch 7, 3 s c in next loop, ch 7, 3 s c in next loop, ch 3, thread over needle, insert in same loop with joining, pull through and work off 2 loops, thread over needle, insert in same loop with joining of next motif, pull through and work off all loops 2 at a time, ch 3, 3 s c in next loop, * ch 7, 3 s c in next loop, repeat from * 18 times, ** thread over needle, insert in next loop (same as joining) pull through and work off 2 loops, thread over needle, insert in same loop with joining of next motif, pull through and work off all loops 2 at a time, ch 3, 3 s c in next loop, * ch 7, 3 s c in next loop, repeat from * 10 times, repeat from ** all around working all corner motifs same as 1st corner motif.

2nd Row—Sl st into loop, ch 4, cluster st in same space, * ch 5, sl st in 4th st from hook for picot, ch 1, cluster st in same space, repeat from * twice, ch 5, 2 s c in next loop, ch 4, sl st in top of last s c for picot, 2 s c in next ch 7 loop of next motif, ** ch 5, 4 cluster sts with ch 1, picot, ch 1 between each cluster st in next loop, * ch 7, 2 s c in next loop, ch 4, sl st in top of last s c for picot, s c in same space, repeat from * twice, repeat from ** 3 times, ch 5, 4 cluster sts with ch 1, picot, ch 1 between each cluster st in next loop, ch 5, 2 s c in next loop, ch 4, sl st in top of last s c for picot, 2 s c in next ch 7 loop of next motif and continue all around in same manner.

If napkins are desired, cut linen the size required. Work a row of s c over a rolled hem.

2nd Row—Ch 7, skip 5 s c, 1 s c in each of the next 3 s c, repeat from beginning all around.

3rd Row—Same as last row of edging on cloth working the 4 cluster sts at corners only.

Chrysanthemum Tablecloth

Materials Required—

AMERICAN THREAD COMPANY
"STAR" MERCERIZED CROCHET COTTON.

ARTICLE 20. SIZE 30

40—325 yd. Balls White, Ecru or Cream or "Gem" Mercerized Crochet Cotton, Article 35, Size 30.

33—400 yd. Balls.

Steel Crochet Hook #12.

Each motif measures about 3 inches. 567 motifs, 21x27 are required for a cloth measuring about 63x81 inches.

MOTIF—Ch 12, join to form a ring, ch 3, * thread over, insert in ring, pull through and work off 2 loops, repeat from *, then work off remaining loops at one time, ** ch 4, * thread over needle, insert in ring, pull through and work off 2 loops, repeat from * twice, thread over and work off remaining loops at one time (this is a cluster stitch), repeat from ** until there are 8 cluster sts in ring, ch 4, join.

2nd Row—Ch 6, sl st in 4th st from hook for picot, ch 7, sl st in 4th st from hook for picot, ch 2, s c in next cluster st, repeat from beginning all around, join.

3rd Row—Sl st to center of picot loop, * ch 9, s c in center of next picot loop, repeat from * all around, join.

4th Row—Sl st into loop, ch 3 and work 3 cluster sts with ch 3 between each cluster st in same loop, * ch 6, 3 cluster sts with ch 3 between each cluster st in next loop, repeat from * all around, ch 6, join in 1st cluster st.

5th Row—Sl st in ch 3 loop, ch 3, work 2 cluster sts with ch 3 between in same loop, ch 3, 2 cluster sts with ch 3 between in next loop, * ch 6, skip 1 loop, 2 cluster sts with ch 3 between in next loop, ch 3, 2 cluster sts with ch 3 between in next loop, repeat from * all around, ch 6, join.

6th Row—Sl st into loop, ch 3 and work 2 cluster sts with ch 3 between in same loop, * ch 3, 2 cluster sts with ch 3 between in next loop, repeat from * once, ** ch 4, s c over the ch 6 loops of 2 previous rows, ch 4, 2 cluster sts with ch 3 between in next ch 3 loop, * ch 3, 2 cluster sts with ch 3 between in next loop, repeat from * once, then repeat from ** all around, join in 1st cluster st.

7th Row—Ch 1, * 2 s c, 4 ch picot, 1 s c in each 3 ch loop, ch 6, sl st in 4th st from hook for picot, ch 2, skip the 2-ch 4 loops, repeat from * all around, join, break thread.

Work another motif in same manner joining it to 1st motif in last row as follows: work 2 s c in 1st ch 3 loop, ch 2, sl st in corresponding picot of 1st motif, ch 2, complete picot, 1 s c in same loop of 2nd motif, join the next 4 picots of 2nd motif in same manner and complete motif same as 1st motif. Join 3rd motif to 2nd motif and join 4th motif to 3rd and 1st motifs in same manner leaving 7 picots free between joinings.

JOINING MOTIF—Work 1st row of large motif, * ch 5, join to 3rd free picot of large motif, ch 2, sl st in 3rd st of ch to complete picot, ch 5, skip 1 picot, sl st in next picot of same large motif, ch 2, sl st in 3rd st of ch to complete picot, ch 2, s c in next cluster st of small motif, ch 6, sl st in 4th st from hook for picot, ch 2, s c in next cluster st of small motif, repeat from * all around joining all motifs in same manner, break thread.

Filet Luncheon Set

Materials Required—AMERICAN THREAD COMPANY "STAR" OR "GEM" MERCERIZED CROCHET COTTON Size 20

4 400-yd. Balls or 9 150-yd. Balls.

Steel Crochet Hook No. 11 or 12.

Each doily measures about 11x15 inches.

Starting at arrow marked A, ch 51 and work 1 d c in the 9th st from hook, 1 d c in each of the next 3 chs, ch 2, skip 2 chs, 1 d c in the next 4 chs, ch 2, skip 2 chs, 1 d c in the next ch, ch 2, skip 2 chs, 1 d c in next ch, then work 27 d c on remainder of ch, ch 3, turn.

2nd Row—Work 1 d c in each of the next 3 d c, ch 2, skip 2 d c, 1 d c in next d c, continue until you have 7 o m (open meshes), 1 s m (solid mesh), 3 o m, 1 s m, 1 o m, 1 s m, ch 2, tr c in the same st as the last d c, ch 5, turn.

3rd Row—1 d c in tr c, 2 d c in ch, 1 d c in next d c, 1 o m, 1 s m, 4 o m, 1 s m, 3 o m, 1 s m, ch 3, turn.

4th Row—1 s m, 2 o m, 1 s m, 1 o m, 1 s m, 2 o m, 1 s m, 5 o m, 1 s m, 1 o m, 1 s m, ch 2, tr c in the same st as last d c, ch 5, turn.

5th Row—1 s m, 1 o m, 1 s m, 3 o m, 1 s m, 2 o m, 1 s m, 1 o m, 1 s m, 3 o m, 1 s m, 1 o m, 1 s m, ch 3, turn.

Continue working back and forth according to diagram to arrow marked B.

Next Row—Omit the last 3 d c in the solid row of insertion, ch 5 for turning, continue to arrow C and continue work on scallop only, complete the scallop and break thread. Join thread in the 4th solid mesh from point of scallop, ch 5, working into side of edging work 1 s m, 1 o m, 1 s m, d c into the next d c on the 11 open mesh row, ch 2, 1 d c into the next d c and work back on the scallop again, you are working on the second side of edging. When you reach the solid row

where one solid mesh was omitted, work a solid mesh into side of work to complete row.

Continue work until there are 8 squares, work corner, then work 4 squares and work other half to correspond joining the work in the last 2 rows by working 1st into the last row then into the 1st row until entire side is joined.

Edging. Join at any point and work * 2 s c, ch 3, 2 s c, ch 3, 2 s c, ch 3, 2 s c in ch 5 loop, 2 s c, ch 3, 2 s c in ch 3 loop, 2 s c, ch 3, 2 s c in next ch 3 loop, 2 s c, ch 3, 2 s c in next 3 ch loop, 2 s c between scallops, 2 s c, ch 3, 2 s c in each of the next 3 loops, repeat from * all around.

Fit a piece of material into the square, allowing for a narrow hem. Over a narrow hem work a row of s c and attach edging using the same crochet thread.

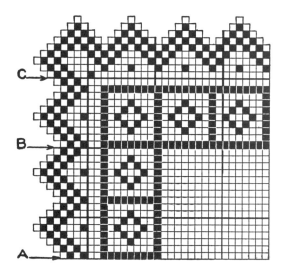

Daisy Ring Tablecloth

MATERIALS — Lily MERCROCHET Cotton size 20:—52-balls White, Cream or Ecru. DAISY Mercerized Crochet Cotton may be substituted if preferred. Crochet hook No. 12. Size—63 x 84 inches.

Block measures 3½ inches point to point.

BLOCK—Ch 8, join with sl st to form ring. *ROW 1*—Ch 6, dc in ring, (ch 3, dc in ring) 6 times, working over starting end to cover it up, ch 3, join with sl st in 3d ch of ch-6. *ROW 2*—Ch 1, sc in same st, (3 sc in next sp, sc in dc) repeated around. Join with sl st in back lp of 1st sc. *ROW 3*—Ch 5, 3 tr in same st, (ch 7, sk 3 sc, 4 tr in back lp of next sc) 7 times, ch 7, sl st in top of ch-5. *ROW 4*—Ch 5, holding back the last lp of each tr on hook, make tr in back lps on next 3 tr, thread over and draw thru all lps on hook (Cluster made), * ch 6, dc in 4th (center) ch of next ch-7 lp, ch 6, (tr in back lps of next 4 tr) made into a Cluster. Repeat from * around. Join to 1st Cluster. *ROW 5*—Ch 3, * 6 dc in next sp, dc in dc,

ch 6, sl st in last dc for a p, 6 dc in next sp, dc in Cluster, ch 6, sl st in one lp on 4th ch from hook for a p, ch 5, p in same way, ** ch 11, p, ch 5, p, ch 3, sl st in last dc (p-lp made). 6 dc in next sp, dc in dc, ch 6, sl st in last dc for a p, 6 dc in next sp, dc in Cluster, a ch-4 p. Repeat from * around. End with sl st in top of ch-3, ch 4, sl st in same st. Cut 6" long, thread to a needle and fasten off on back.

2d BLOCK—Repeat to ** in Row 5. Ch 3, sl st in one lp of center ch at tip of a p-lp on 1st Block, ch 7, p, ch 5, p, ch 3, sl st back in last dc on 2d Block. * 6 dc in next sp, dc in dc, ch 3, sl st in next ch-6 p on 1st Block, ch 3, sl st back in last dc on 2d Block, 6 dc in next sp, dc in Cluster, * ch 2, sl st in next ch-4 p on 1st Block, ch 2, sl st back in last dc. Repeat from * to *. Ch 6, p, ch 5, p, ch 3, sl st in one lp of center ch of next p-lp on 1st Block, ch 7, p, ch 5, p, ch 3, sl st back in last dc. Complete as for 1st Block. Join 3rd Block to 2d Block and 4th Block to 1st and 3d Blocks in same way.

Following illustration make 823 Blocks and join 18 x 24 around outside. Stretch and pin cloth right-side-down on quilting or curtain frames. Lay frames over an ironing board or padded table a section at a time, steaming and pressing dry each section thru a cloth until completely blocked.

21

Tulip Tablecloth

Materials Required—

AMERICAN THREAD COMPANY
"STAR" MERCERIZED CROCHET COTTON.
ARTICLE 20. SIZE 20

48—250 yd. Balls White, Ecru or Cream or "Gem" Mercerized Crochet Cotton, Article 35, Size 20.
40—300 yd. Balls.
Steel Crochet Hook #11.

Each motif measures about 6 inches. 176 motifs 11x16 are required for cloth measuring 66x96 inches.

LARGE MOTIF—Ch 8, join to form a ring, ch 4, * thread over twice, insert in ring, pull through and work off 2 loops twice, repeat from *, thread over and work off all loops at one time, ** ch 4, * thread over twice, insert in ring, pull through and work off 2 loops twice, repeat from * twice, thread over and work off all loops at one time (a cluster st), repeat from ** 6 times, ch 4, join in 1st cluster st.

2nd Row—Ch 4, tr c in same space, ch 7, 2 tr c in same space, * ch 3, 2 tr c, ch 7, 2 tr c in next cluster st, repeat from * all around, ch 3, join in 4th st of ch.

3rd Row—Sl st to center of loop, ** ch 5, 2 tr c in 1st st of ch, * ch 4, 2 tr c in top of last tr c, (rice st) repeat from * 7 times, s c in top of 4th rice st, ch 4, 2 tr c in same space, ch 4, 2 tr c in top of last tr c, s c in top of 2nd rice st, ch 4, 2 tr c in same space, ch 4, 2 tr c in top of last tr c, skip one loop, s c in next loop, repeat from ** all around, break thread.

4th Row—Join thread between 5th and 6th rice sts, ch 12, d c between next 2 rice sts, * ch 9, d c between next 2 rice sts, repeat from *, ** ch 9, s c between 10th and 11th rice sts, ch 7, tr c between 12th and 13th rice sts, tr c between 1st and 2nd rice sts of next group, ch 7, s c between 3rd and 4th rice sts, ch 9, d c between 5th and 6th rice sts, * ch 9, d c between next 2 rice sts, repeat from * twice, repeat from ** 6 times, ch 9, s c between 10th and 11 rice sts,

ch 7, tr c between 12th and 13th rice sts, tr c between 1st and 2nd rice sts of 1st group, ch 7, s c between 3rd and 4th rice sts, ch 9, join in 3rd st of ch.

5th Row—Sl st to loop, ch 3, 2 d c in same space, ch 3, 3 d c, ch 3, 3 d c in same space, ** ch 3, 3 d c, ch 3, 3 d c, ch 3, 3 d c, ch 3, 3 d c in next loop, * ch 3, 3 d c, ch 3, 3 d c, ch 3, 3 d c in next loop, repeat from *, s c in next loop, ch 3, s c in next 7 ch loop, 3 d c, ch 3, 3 d c, ch 3, 3 d c in next loop, ch 3, 3 d c, ch 3, 3 d c, ch 3, 3 d c in next loop, repeat from ** 6 times, ch 3, 3 d c, ch 3, 3 d c, ch 3, 3 d c, ch 3, 3 d c in next loop, * ch 3, 3 d c, ch 3, 3 d c, ch 3, 3 d c in next loop, repeat from *, s c in next loop, ch 3, s c in next 7 ch loop, 3 d c, ch 3, 3 d c, ch 3, 3 d c in next loop, ch 3, join in 3rd st of ch.

6th Row—Sl st to center of next loop, * ch 5, s c in next loop, repeat from * 10 times, ** skip next 3 ch loop, s c in next 3 ch loop, ch 2, sl st in last 5 ch loop of previous scallop, ch 2, s c in next 3 ch loop of 2nd scallop, ch 2, sl st in next 5 ch loop of previous scallop, ch 2, s c in next 3 ch loop of 2nd scallop, * ch 5, s c in next loop, repeat from * 11 times, repeat from ** 6 times, skip next 3 ch loop, s c in next 3 ch loop, ch 2, sl st in last 5 ch loop of previous scallop, ch 2, s c in next 3 ch loop of 1st scallop, ch 2, sl st in next 5 ch loop of previous scallop, ch 2, s c in next 3 ch loop of 1st scallop, ch 3, d c in sl st of 1st loop, (this brings thread in position for next row).

7th Row—Ch 3, s c in next loop, * ch 7, sl st in 5th st from hook for picot, ch 2, 2 d c in next loop, repeat from * 5 times, ch 7, sl st in 5th st from hook for picot, ch 2, s c in next loop, ch 3, s c in next loop, ch 6, sl st in 5th st from hook for picot, ch 1, s c in next loop of next scallop, repeat from beginning all around, break thread.

Work a 2nd motif in same manner joining to 1st motif in last row as follows: ch 3, s c in next loop, * ch 7, sl st in 5th st from hook for picot, ch 2, 2 d c in next loop, repeat from * twice, * ch 5, sl st in corresponding picot of 1st motif, ch 2, complete picot, ch 2, 2 d c in next loop of 2nd motif, repeat from * twice, ch 7, sl st in 5th st from hook for picot, ch 2, s c in next loop, ch 3, s c in next loop, ch 6, sl st in 5th st from hook for picot, ch 1, s c in next loop, ch 3, s c in next loop, ch 7, sl st in 5th st from hook for picot, ch 2, 2 d c in next loop, * ch 5, sl st in corresponding picot of 1st motif, ch 2, complete picot, ch 2, 2 d c in next loop of 2nd motif, repeat from * twice and complete motif same as 1st motif, break thread. Join 3rd motif to 2nd motif and 4th motif to 3rd and 1st motifs in same manner.

JOINING MOTIF—Work 1st 2 rows same as large motif.
3rd Row—Work 2 rice sts, ch 2, sl st in center free picot of 1st scallop, ch 2, complete picot, work 2 rice sts, skip next loop of joining motif, s c in next loop, work 2 rice sts, ch 2, sl st in center free picot of next scallop of same motif, ch 2, complete picot, work 2 rice sts, skip next loop of joining motif, s c in next loop, work 2 rice sts, ch 2, sl st in center free picot of next scallop of next motif, ch 2, complete picot and continue in same manner until joining is completed, break thread.

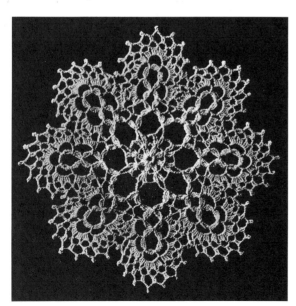

Sunset

Materials: Clark's O.N.T. Mercerized Crochet, size 30, 16 balls of Ecru and 7 balls of color Dk. Yellow; or J. & P. Coats Mercerized Crochet, 12 balls of Ecru and 5 balls of Dk. Yellow; or if Clark's Big Ball Mercerized Crochet is being used, buy 6 balls of Ecru only. Milward's steel crochet hook No. 8.

½ yd. 54 inch width natural linen for 4 napkins. Set consists of 4 place mats each about 11 x 21 inches, a center mat about 13 x 28 inches, and 4 napkins each 13 inches square. The center mesh of mat is worked first, then sunset patterns are worked and sewed to each end.

Place Mat. Center Mesh: With Ecru, ch 162, turn. **1st row:** D c in 8th ch from hook, d c in each ch across (155 d c). Ch 8, turn. **2nd row:** D c in each d c across. Ch 8, turn. **3rd row:** D c in each of first 5 d c (thus making a loop on edge), * ch 1, skip 2 d c, d c in next d c, ch 1, skip 2 d c, d c in next d c, ch 2, d c in next d c, repeat from * across, ending row with ch 1, skip 2 d c, d c in each of next 5 d c. Ch 8, turn. **4th row:** D c in each first 5 d c (thus making a loop on edge), d c in next single d c, ch 2, d c in same single d c, * ch 1, d c in next ch-2, ch 1, d c in next single d c, ch 2, d c in same single d c, repeat from * across, ending row with d c in last single d c, ch 2, d c in same single d c, d c in each of last 5 d c. Ch 8, turn. **5th row:** D c in each of first 5 d c, * ch 1, d c in next ch-2 sp, ch 1, d c in next single d c, ch 2, d c in same single d c, repeat from * across, ending row with d c in last ch-2 sp, ch 1, d c in each of last 5 d c. Ch 8, turn. Repeat 4th and 5th rows alternately, until work measures 11 inches. Then work 2 rows of d c to correspond with the beginning. Do not break off thread but continue for edging along long side as follows:

Edging. 1st row: * Ch 3, 3 d c with ch 3 between each d c in next loop, ch 3, 2 s c in next loop, repeat from * across, ending row with 3 d c with ch 3 between in last loop, ch 3, sl st to base of last d c of 1st row. Ch 3, turn. **2nd row:** * S c in ch-3 loop, s c in d c, ch 5, s c in next loop, s c in next loop, ch 5, s c in next d c, s c in next loop, ch 2 (this ch-2 should come directly over 2-s c of previous row), repeat from * across, ending row with s c in last d c, sl st along last ch-3 loop. Turn and break off. **3rd row:** Attach Dk. Yellow, make 4 s c in ch-3 loop, * 9 s c in ch-5 loop, 4 s c in next ch-5 loop, ch 5, remove hook, insert hook in 5th s c of ch-5 loop just completed, draw loop through, 9 s c in ch-5 loop, 5 s c in next incompleted loop, 3 s c in ch-2 loop, repeat from * across, ending row to correspond with beginning. Break off. Work edging on opposite side in same way.

Sunset Pattern: With Ecru, ch 6, join with sl st to form ring. **1st row:** Ch 6, d c in ring, * ch 3, d c in ring, repeat from * until 4 loops are made. Ch 8, turn. **2nd row:** D c in 1st loop, * ch 5, d c in next loop, repeat from * until 4 loops are made, then ch 5, d c in 4th st of turning ch. Ch 8, turn. **3rd row:** D c in first loop, * ch 8, d c in next loop, repeat from * until 5 loops are made. Ch 7, turn. **4th row:** D c in 4th st of first ch-8 loop, * ch 6, d c in 3rd st of next ch-8 loop, ch 4, skip 2 ch, d c in next ch of same ch-8 loop, repeat from * until 9 loops are made. Ch 6, turn. **5th row:** * D c in next d c, ch 6, repeat from * until 8 loops are made, then ch 3, d c in 3rd st of turning ch. Ch 3, turn. **6th row:** D c in each ch st and d c in each d c of previous row (57 d c, counting turning ch-3 as 1 d c). Ch 3, turn. **7th row:** D c in each of next 3 d c, * ch 2, d c in each of next 7 d c, repeat from * across, ending with ch 2, d c in each of last 4 d c (7 groups of 7-d c and 2 groups of 4-d c). Ch 3, turn. **8th row:** D c in each d c and ch 3 (instead of ch 2) between d c-groups. Ch 3, turn. **9th to 15th rows incl:** Work d c in each d c, making 1 additional ch st in the ch-loops between the d c-groups. (There

will be ch 10 between d c-groups on 15th row.) At end of 15th row, turn and break off. **16th row:** Attach Dk. Yellow and make s c in each d c of 4-d c group, ch 18, ** sl st in 2nd d c of next 7-d c group, turn, s c in 1st st of ch-18, 1 half d c in next st, d c in each of next 2 sts, tr in each of next 3 sts, d c in each of next 2 sts, 1 half d c in next st, s c in next st (a petal made), * ch 17, turn, sl st in next d c of same 7-d c group, turn and make another petal in same way, repeat from * until 5 petals are made. Then ch 7, s c in each d c of next 7-d c group, ch 18, repeat from ** across, ending row with ch 7, s c in each of last 4 d c. Turn and break off. **17th row:** Attach Ecru, s c in each of first 3 s c, * 10 s c in next ch-loop. In each of next 4 loops (between petals) make 1 s c, 1 half d c, 2 d c, 5 tr, 2 d c, 1 half d c and 1 s c (1 shell made). Then 10 s c in next ch-loop, skip 1st s c of 7-s c group, s c in each of next 5 s c. Repeat from * across, ending row with s c in each of last 3 s c. Ch 7, turn.

18th row: Skip 4 s c of first loop, s c in next s c, ch 3, skip 3 sts of next shell, d c in next st, * ch 5, skip 1 st, d c in next st, repeat from * twice more, holding back on hook the last 2 loops of the last d c; then skip 3 sts of next shell, d c in next st, working off 2 loops, then thread over hook and draw thread through all loops on hook. Repeat from first * across the next 3 shells of this group completing the last d c on 4th shell, then ch 5, s c in center s c of next s c-loop, ch 7, s c in center s c of next s c-loop, ch 5, skip 3 sts of next shell, and continue thus across, ending row with ch 3, tr in last s c. Ch 7, turn. **19th row:** Skip first 2 loops, 2 s c in next ch-5 loop, * ch 3, 3 d c with ch 3 between d c's in next loop, ch 3, 2 s c in next loop, ch 1, 2 s c in next loop, repeat from * across the next 3 shells, after the last 2 s c are made in the 3rd loop of 4th shell, ch 3, skip next loop, d c in 3rd st of ch-7, ch 3, skip next loop, 2 s c in next loop, and continue thus across, ending row with 2 s c in 3rd loop from end, then ch 3, tr in 3rd st of turning ch. Ch 5, turn. **20th row:** 2 s c in first loop, * ch 5, 2 s c in next loop, repeat from * twice more, then ch 2, skip ch-1 sp, 2 s c in next loop, ch 5, 2 s c in next loop, repeat from first * across the next 3 shells, after the last 2 s c are made in the 4th loop of 4th shell, make 4 s c in next loop, s c in next d c, 4 s c in next loop, 2 s c in next loop, ch 5, and continue thus across, ending row with 3 ch-5 loops after the last ch-2 sp. Turn and break off.

21st row: Attach Dk. Yellow, and * work 9 s c in each of next 2 loops, 5 s c in next loop, ch 5, remove hook, then insert hook in 5th s c of s c-loop just completed and draw loop through, ch 5, remove hook, then insert hook in 5th s c of next s c-loop and draw loop through. Work 9 s c in this loop, 5 s c in next loop, ch 5, remove hook, insert hook in 5th s c of s c-loop to the right and draw loop through, work 9 s c in this loop, 4 s c in next incompleted loop, 4 s c in next incompleted loop, s c in ch-2 sp. Repeat from * across, making 7 s c over group of 9-s c between groups. Break off. This completes sunset pattern for one end. Make another one same as this

Continued on page 27

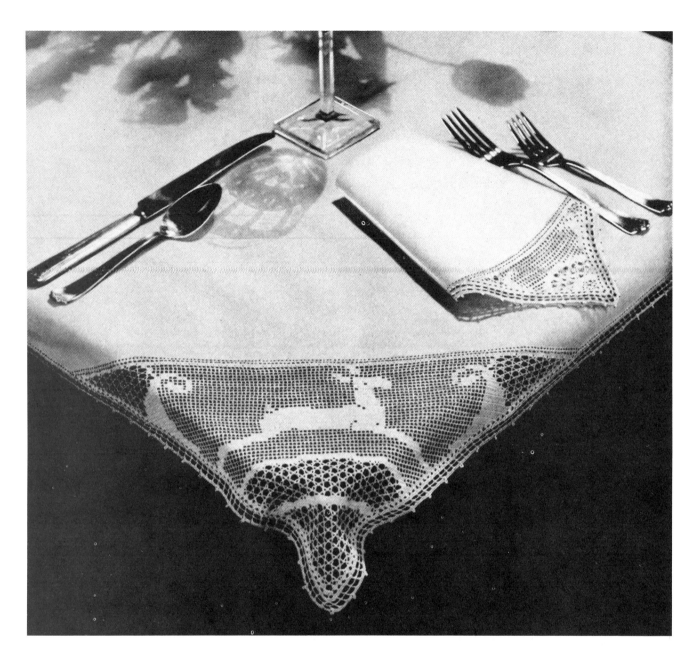

Gazelle Luncheon Set

Materials: Choose one of the following threads in White or Ecru:

> Clark's O.N.T. Mercerized Crochet, size 80, 5 balls.
>
> J. & P. Coats Mercerized Crochet, size 80, 3 balls.
>
> Milward's steel crochet hook No. 9 or 10.
>
> 1¾ yards of 39 inch linen.

When completed, luncheon set measures about 38x38 inches, and each napkin about 12 inches square.

Beginning at point directly below gazelle, ch 8. **1st row:** D c in 5th ch from hook, ch 2, skip 2 ch, d c in last ch, ch 7, turn. **2nd row:** D c in d c from which ch-7 started, 2 d c in sp, d c in next d c, 2 d c in next sp, d c in 3rd st of turning ch, ch 2, tr in same st with last d c, ch 7, turn. **3rd row:** D c in tr, 2 d c in sp, d c in 1st d c of 7-d c, ch 5, d c in last d c of 7-d c,

2 d c in next sp, d c in 3rd st of turning ch, ch 2, tr in same st with last d c, ch 7, turn.

4th row: D c in tr, 2 d c in sp, d c in next d c, ch 2, skip 2 d c, d c in next d c, ch 3, skip 2 sts of ch-5, sl st in next st, ch 3, skip next 2 sts of same ch-5, d c in next d c, ch 2, skip 2 d c, d c in next d c, 2 d c in next sp, d c in 3rd st, ch 2, tr in same st with last d c, ch 7, turn. Work in this manner, following chart, increasing sps at beginning and end of rows. Make 4 corners.

Edging: Cut corners of cloth so that crocheted pieces can be put on as in illustration. Have edges of cloth hemstitched. Sew on crocheted corners and make edging as follows: **1st row:** Attach thread to a hemstitched sp and make 2 s c in each sp around cloth and 4 s c in each sp of crocheted corner. Ch 7, turn.

2nd row: * Skip 3 s c, d c in next s c, ch 3, repeat from * around, ch 7, turn. **3rd row:** Work sp over sp, ch 2, turn. **4th row:** 3 s c in each sp and 1 s c in each d c, making a ch-5 p in every 3rd d c.

Napkins: Start same as for corners of cloth, and then follow chart. Make edging same as for cloth.

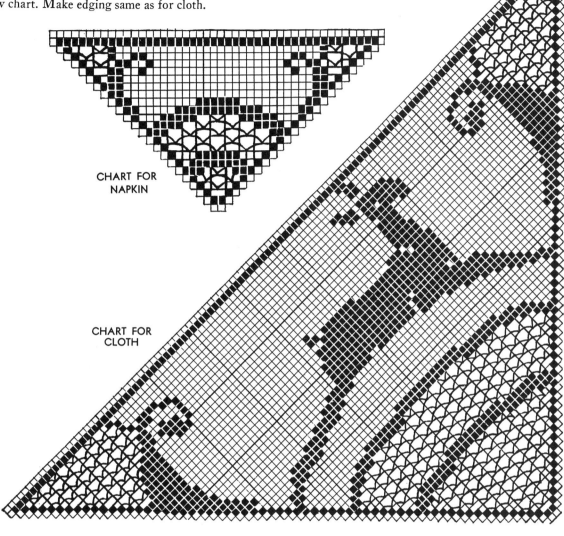

CHART FOR
NAPKIN

CHART FOR
CLOTH

Sunset

Continued from page 25

and sew one to each end of place mat with over and over stitches. Make 3 more place mats.

Center Mat. Start center mesh with ch 190 and work as for place mat until piece measures 14½ inches. Then work 2 rows of d c to correspond with beginning. To make sunset pattern, starting with Ecru ch 6, join with sl st to form ring. **1st row:** Ch 6, d c in ring, * ch 3, d c in ring, repeat from * until 5 loops are made. Ch 8, turn. **2nd to 6th rows incl:** Work as for 2nd to 6th rows incl. of mesh pattern on place mat, excepting that there will be 6 loops in 2nd row; 6 loops in 3rd row; 11 loops in 4th row; 11 loops in 5th row; 71 d c in 6th row. Continue as for mesh pattern on place mat. (There will be 9 groups of 7-d c, and 2 groups of 4-d c.) Make another one same as this and sew one to each end of center mat.

Napkins. Cut linen 13 inches square. Make a ¼ inch hem around edges. **1st row:** Attach Yellow to one corner of napkin and make ch-5 loops all around, spacing loops evenly and making an even number of loops on each side. Join and break off. **2nd row:** Attach thread to 2nd loop before next corner and make 9 s c in same loop, 9 s c in each of next 2 loops, 5 s c in next loop, * ch 5, remove hook, insert hook in 5th s c of next s c-loop (to the right) and draw loop through, repeat from * 2 more times (3 loops made), make 9 s c in loop just made, 9 s c in next loop, 9 s c in next loop, 4 s c in incompleted loop (this completes corner), ** 9 s c in next loop, 5 s c in next loop, ch 5, remove hook, insert hook in 5th s c of s c-loop (to the right) and draw loop through, 9 s c in this loop, 4 s c in next incompleted loop. Repeat from ** across, making each corner as corner just made.

Lily of the Valley Tablecloth

Materials Required—

AMERICAN THREAD COMPANY

"STAR" MERCERIZED CROCHET COTTON.

ARTICLE 20. SIZE 30

36—325 yd. Balls White, Ecru or Cream or "Gem" Mercerized Crochet Cotton, Article 35, Size 30.
30—400 yd. Balls.
Steel Crochet Hook #12.

Each motif measures about 3 inches. 567 motifs 21x27 are required for cloth measuring about 63x81 inches without edge.

MOTIF—Ch 8, join to form a ring, ch 4 and work 23 tr c into ring, join in 4th st of ch.

2nd Row—Ch 3, d c in same space, * ch 6, sl st in 5th st from hook for picot, ch 6, sl st in 5th st from hook for picot, ch 1, skip 2 tr c, 2 d c in next tr c, repeat from * 6 times, * ch 6, sl st in 5th st from hook for picot, repeat from *, ch 1, join in 3rd st of ch.

3rd Row—Ch 4, tr c in d c, * ch 6, sl st in 5th st from hook for picot, repeat from * 3 times, ch 1, 1 tr c in each of the next 2 d c, repeat from 1st * all around in same manner, join in 4th st of ch.

4th Row—Ch 10, * tr c in center of 4 picot loop, ch 6, tr c between next 2 tr c, ch 6, tr c in same space, ch 6, tr c in center of next 4 picot loop, ch 6, tr c between next 2 tr c, ch 6, repeat from * twice, tr c in center of next 4 picot loop, ch 6, tr c between next 2 tr c, ch 6, tr c in same space, ch 6, tr c in center of next 4 picot loop, ch 6, join in 4th st of ch.

5th Row—Ch 1, 6 s c over loop, ch 5, s c in next loop, ch 5, 3 d c in next loop, ch 3, 3 d c in same loop, * ch 5, s c in next loop, ch 5, 6 s c over each of the next 2 loops, ch 5, s c in next loop, ch 5, 3 d c in next loop, ch 3, 3 d c in same loop, repeat from * twice, ch 5, s c in next loop, ch 5, 6 s c over next loop, join in 1st s c.

6th Row—Ch 1, 1 s c in each of the next 4 s c, * ch 5, s c in next loop, repeat from * once, ** ch 5, 1 d c in each d c, 3 tr c in corner space, ch 3, 1 d c in each d c, * ch 5, s c in next loop, repeat from *, ch 5, skip 2 s c, 1 s c in each of the next 8 s c, * ch 5, s c in next loop, repeat from * once, then repeat from ** all around in same manner ending row with skip 2 s c, 1 s c in each of the next 4 s c, join in 1st s c.

7th Row—Ch 1, 1 s c in each of the next 2 s c, * ch 5, s c in next loop, repeat from * twice, ** ch 5, 1 d c in each of the next 6 sts, 3 tr c in corner loop, ch 5, 3 tr c in same loop, 1 d c in each of the next 6 sts, * ch 5, s c in next loop, repeat from * twice, ch 5, skip 2 s c, 1 s c in each of the next 4 s c, * ch 5, s c in next loop, repeat from * twice, then repeat from ** all around in same manner, join in 1st s c, break thread.

Work a 2nd motif in same manner joining to 1st motif in last row as follows: ch 1, 1 s c in each of the next 2 s c, * ch 5, s c in next loop, repeat from * twice, ch 5, 1 d c in each of the next 6 sts, 3 tr c in corner loop, ch 2, sl st in corresponding loop of 1st motif, 3 tr c in same loop of 2nd

motif, 1 d c in each of the next 6 sts, * ch 2, sl st in corresponding loop of 1st motif, ch 2, s c in next loop of 2nd motif, repeat from * twice, ch 2, sl st in corresponding loop of 1st motif, ch 2, skip 2 s c of 2nd motif, 1 s c in each of the next 4 s c, * ch 2, sl st in corresponding loop of 1st motif, ch 2, s c in next loop of 2nd motif, repeat from * twice, ch 2, sl st in corresponding loop of 1st motif, ch 2, 1 d c in each of the next 6 sts of 2nd motif, 3 tr c in corner loop, ch 2, sl st in corresponding loop of 1st motif, ch 2, 3 tr c in same loop of 2nd motif and complete motif same as 1st motif. Join 3rd motif to 2nd motif and 4th motif to 1st and 3rd motifs in same manner.

EDGE: With right side of work toward you and starting at corner motif, join thread in center of s c group to the right of corner, * ch 5, s c in next loop, repeat from * 3 times, ch 5, skip 4 d c, s c in next d c, ch 5, 3 tr c in corner loop, ch 5, 3 tr c in same loop, ** ch 5, skip 3 tr c and 1 d c, s c in next d c, * ch 5, s c in next loop, repeat from * 3 times, ch 5, s c in center of s c group, * ch 5, s c in next loop, repeat from * 3 times, ch 5, skip 4 d c, s c in next d c, * ch 5, s c in next loop, repeat from *, then repeat from ** all around working all corners in same manner, join.

2nd Row—Sl st to center of loop, ch 8, sl st in 5th st from hook for picot, d c in next loop, * ch 5, sl st in 5th st from hook for picot, d c in next loop, repeat from * twice, * ch 5, sl st in 5th st from hook for picot, ch 6, sl st in 5th st from hook for picot, d c in next loop, repeat from * once, ch 5, sl st in 5th st from hook for picot, * ch 6, sl st in 5th st from hook for picot, repeat from * once, d c in same loop (corner), * ch 5, sl st in 5th st from hook for picot, ch 6, sl st in 5th st from hook for picot, d c in next loop, repeat from * once, * ch 5, sl st in 5th st from hook for picot, d c in next loop, repeat from * 10 times, ch 5, sl st in 5th st from hook for picot, d c in same loop, ** ch 5, sl st in 5th st from hook for picot, d c in next loop, * ch 5, sl st in 5th st from hook for picot, d c in next loop, repeat from * 11 times, ch 5, sl st in 5th st from hook for picot, d c in same loop, repeat from ** all around working all corners same as 1st corner.

If napkins are desired, cut linen the size required. Turn under a small hem. Work a row of s c all around.

2nd Row—Ch 7, sl st in 5th st from hook for picot, ch 2, skip 3 s c, s c in next s c, repeat from beginning all around.

Rose Filet Cloth

Materials Required—
AMERICAN THREAD COMPANY
"STAR" MERCERIZED CROCHET COTTON.
ARTICLE 20. SIZE 30

30—325 yd. Balls White, Cream or Ecru.
3 yds of 36 inch Linen will be required for a cloth measuring
about 68 x 103 inches.
Steel Crochet Hook No. 12.

Gauge: 6 mesh = 1 inch

Ch 200, d c in 8th st from hook, 1 d c in each of the next
3 sts of ch, * ch 2, skip 2 sts of ch, d c in next st, repeat
from * 14 times, 1 d c in each of the next 3 sts of ch, * ch 2,
skip 2 sts of ch, d c in next st, repeat from * 24 times, 1
d c in each of the next 3 sts of ch, * ch 2, skip 2 sts of ch,
d c in next st, repeat from * 18 times, 1 d c in each of
the next 3 sts of ch, ch 2, skip 2 sts of ch, d c in last st,
ch 5 to turn each row.

2nd Row—D c in next d c, 1 d c in each of the next 3 d c,
* ch 2, d c in next d c, repeat from * 18 times, 1 d c in
each of the next 3 d c (a solid mesh), * 2 d c in mesh, 1
d c in next d c, repeat from * once, * ch 2, d c in next d c
(an open mesh), repeat from * 22 times, 1 d c in each of
the next 3 d c, * ch 2, d c in next d c, repeat from * 14
times, 1 d c in each of the next 3 d c, ch 2, d c in 3rd st
of ch.

3rd Row—1 open mesh, 1 solid mesh, 15 open meshes, 1
solid mesh, 22 open meshes, 2 solid meshes, 21 open meshes,
1 solid mesh, 1 open mesh. Continue working back and forth
according to diagram to arrow, then repeat from beginning
to arrow 6 times.

Work 2 more lengths of insertion in same manner and finish
all edges with a row of s c, working 2 s c in 1 mesh and 3
s c in next mesh and 5 s c in each corner mesh.

Cut 2 strips of linen 4 inches wide and required length. Cut
2 strips of linen 14 inches wide and required length. Work
a row of s c over a narrow rolled hem around linen sections.
Sew linen and insertion together as illustrated.

EDGE: Join thread in corner, * 1 s c in each of the next 12
s c, ch 5, turn, s c in 6th s c from hook, ch 5, s c in 1st
s c made, ch 1, turn and work 9 s c over first ch 5 loop and
5 s c over 2nd loop, ch 5, turn, s c in center st of 1st scallop,
ch 1, turn and work 5 s c over loop, ch 3, slip st in top of
s c for picot, 4 s c over same loop, sl st in top of 2nd
scallop and finish same scallop with 4 more s c, slip st into
s c of previous row, repeat from * all around, break thread.
If napkins to match are desired, cut squares of linen the size
required and work a row of s c over a narrow rolled hem.

EDGE: Starting at corner, * 1 s c in each of the next 6 s c,
ch 5, turn, s c in 1st s c, ch 1, turn, work 3 s c over loop,
ch 3, slip st in top of s c for picot, 3 s c over same loop,
repeat from * all around, break thread.

FILET CROCHET INSTRUCTIONS

OPEN MESH

When worked on a chain, work the first d c in 8th ch
from hook * ch 2, skip 2 sts, 1 d c in next st, repeat from *.
Succeeding rows, ch 5 to turn and d c in d c, * ch 2, d c
in next d c, repeat from *.

SOLID MESH

Four double crochets form 1 solid mesh and 3 d c are
required for each additional solid mesh.

To increase a solid mesh at end of row, work a tr c in same
space with last d c, work 2 more tr c working each tr c
into lower loop of previous st.

To increase 1 open mesh at end of row, ch 2, tr c in same
space with last d c.

To increase 1 open mesh at beginning of row, ch 8, d c
in 1st d c.

To increase a solid mesh at beginning of row, ch 5, 1 d c
in 4th st from hook, 1 d c in next st of ch, d c in next d c.

To decrease a mesh at beginning of row, sl st across 1st
mesh.

Lace Medallion Luncheon Set

MATERIALS — DAISY Mercerized Crochet Cotton size 30:—5-balls or 4 skeins White, Cream or Ecru (sufficient for Centerpiece, 4 Place Mats and 4 Coasters). Crochet hook size 13.

BLOCK—(Size—3½" square) — Ch 7, sl st in 1st st. Ch 9, tr in ring, holding starting end around ring and working over it to cover it up, (ch 4, tr in ring) 6 times, ch 4, sl st in 5th ch of 1st ch-9. **ROW 2**—Ch 1, sc in next ch-4 sp, * (ch 4, sc) twice in same sp, ch 4, sc in next sp. Repeat from * around. End with ch 2, dc in 1st sc drawn down to make lp the same size as others (24 lps). **ROW 3**—(Ch 4, sc in next lp) 23 times, ch 2, dc in next lp. **ROW 4**—Repeat Row 3. **ROW 5**—* Ch 12, sk 1 lp, sc in next lp, (ch 4, sc in next lp) 4 times. Repeat from * around, ending with 3 ch-4 lps, ch 2, dc in next lp. **ROW 6**—* Ch 2, sk 2 ch of next ch-12 lp, (3 sc, ch 4, sl st in last sc for a p) 3 times and 3 sc,—all in lp, leaving final 2 ch of lp uncovered too. Ch 2, sc in next ch-4, lp, (ch 4, sc in next lp) 3 times. Repeat from * around, with ch 2 and dc for final lp. **ROW 7**—* (Ch 12, dc between next 2 ps) twice, ch 12, sc in next ch-4 lp (ch 4, sc in next lp) twice. Repeat from * around, with ch 2 and dc for final lp. **ROW 8**—* Ch 2, sk 1st 2 ch of next ch-12 lp, (4 sc, p) twice and 4 sc all on bal. of lp, (4 sc, p, 6 sc, p, and 4 sc) all in next lp, (4 sc, p) twice and 4 sc all in next lp leaving final 2 ch of lp uncovered, ch 2, sc in next ch-4 lp, ch 4, sc in next lp. Repeat from * around with ch 2 and dc for final lp. **ROW 9**—Ch 18, * dc between next 2 ps, ch 15, dc in 3d sc between ps on next lp, ** ch 21, dc in next sc, ch 15, dc between ps in next lp, ch 13, tr in ch-4 lp at tip of point, ch 13 and repeat from * around. Join with sl st in 5th ch of 1st ch-18. Cut 6" long, thread to a needle and fasten off on back.

2d BLOCK—Repeat to ** in Row 9. Ch 10, sl st in one lp of center (11th) st in a corner lp on 1st Block, ch 10, dc back in next sc on 2d Block, ch 7, sl st in next lp on 1st Block, ch 7, dc back between 2 ps on next lp on 2d Block, ch 6, sl st in next lp on 1st Block, ch 6, tr back in next ch-4 lp on 2d Block, ch 6, sl st in next lp on 1st Block, ch 6, dc back between ps on next lp on 2d Block, ch 7, sl st in next lp on 1st Block, ch 7, **dc back in 3d sc** between ps on next lp on 2d Block, ch 10, sl st in center st on corner lp of 1st Block, ch 10, dc back in

next sc on 2d Block. Complete row as for 1st Block.

PLACE MAT—(Size—11½"x16") — Make and join 12 Blocks 3x4 (or other desired size). **Edge**—Sc in one corner, ch 15, sc in same lp, * ch 15, sc in next lp, (ch 13, sc in next lp) 3 times, ch 15, sc in joining of Blocks. Repeat from * around, with an extra ch-15 lp at corners. **ROW 2**—Ch 1, sc in next (corner) lp, (ch 4, sc in same lp) 5 times, * ch 2, sc in next lp, (ch 4, sc) 4 times in same lp. Repeat from * around with corner lps like 1st one. End with ch 2, sl st in 1st sc. **ROW 3**—Sl st to center of next lp, (ch 4, sc in next lp) twice, ch 5, sc in same last lp, (ch

4, sc in next lp) twice, * ch 1, sc in next ch-4 lp on next scallop, (ch 4, sc in next lp) 3 times. Repeat from * around, with corners like 1st one. Join and fasten off. Repeat for desired number of mats.

CENTERPIECE—(Size — 11½"x23") —Make and join 18 Blocks 3x6. Repeat Edge.

COASTER—Make one Block and repeat Edge around it.

Stretch and pin doilies right-side-down on a padded board in true shape. Steam and press dry thru a cloth.

Bedspreads

Starbright

MATERIALS:

Clark's O.N.T. Mercerized Bedspread Cotton: **Single Size Spread** —72 x 107 inches (including fringe) —54 balls of White, Ecru or Cream, or 78 balls of Bedspread Peach. **Double Size Spread**—88 x 107 inches (including fringe)—76 balls of White, Ecru or Cream, or 108 balls of Bedspread Peach.

Steel Crochet Hook No. 7.

GAUGE: Block measures 4½ inches from side to side.

FIRST BLOCK . . . Starting at center, ch 8. Join with sl st. **1st rnd:** Ch 1, 18 sc in ring. Join with sl st in first sc. **2nd rnd:** Ch 3, dc in next 2 sc, (ch 5, dc in next 3 sc) 5 times; ch 5, sl st in top st of ch-3. **3rd rnd:** Ch 3, dc in next 2 dc, (ch 6, dc in next 3 dc) 5 times; ch 6. Join. **4th rnd:** Ch 3, dc in next 2 dc, (ch 5, sc under next two chains, ch 5, dc in next 3 dc) 5 times; ch 5, sc under next two chains, ch 5.

Continued on page 37

Golden Wedding

MATERIALS: J. & P. COATS BEDSPREAD COTTON, *18 balls of White or Ecru for single size spread; 21 balls for double size spread.*
MILWARD'S *steel crochet hook No. 8.*

GAUGE: 4 sps make 1 inch; 4 rows make 1 inch. Completed motif measures 7½ inches square. For a single size spread, about 75 x 106 inches including fringe, make 9 x 13 motifs. For a double size spread, about 91 x 106 inches including fringe, make 11 x 13 motifs.

MOTIF... Starting at center section, ch 15. **1st row:** D c in 3rd ch from hook and in next 2 ch (these 4 d c make 1 bl); ch 2, skip 2 ch, d c in next ch (sp); make another sp, end with 4 d c (bl). Ch 5, turn. **2nd row:** D c in last d c of bl; make d c in next 2 ch, d c in d c, d c in next 2 ch and in d c. Ch 2, d c in top st of turning ch-3. Ch 5, turn. **3rd row:** Sp over sp and bl over bl. Ch 3, turn. **4th row:** D c in next 2 ch and in d c, 2 sps over next 2 bls, bl over next sp (center section completed). Hereafter work in rnds. **1st rnd:** Ch 5, d c at base of last d c made, ch 2, d c at base of d c (turning ch) of previous row, ch 2, d c at base of next end d c, ch 2, d c at base of next ch-3, ch 5 (corner), d c in same place, sp over next bl. Continue to make sps thus around and ch-5 at corners, ending with ch 5, join with sl st to 3rd ch of ch-5 first made. **2nd rnd:** Ch 5, d c in next d c. Now make sp over each sp around, making an extra ch-5 at each corner. Join. **3rd rnd:** Ch 5 (to count as d c of last bl and ch-2 of 1st sp), d c in next d c; 3 more sps, 7 d c (2 bls); ch 5, another d c in corner ch, 6 more d c, 4 sps, 7 d c. Continue thus around. Join. **4th rnd:** Ch 3, 4 bls over 4 sps, 2 bls over 2 bls, ch 2, d c in 3rd ch of corner ch-5, ch 5, d c in same place, ch 2, d c in next d c, 8 bls, sp, ch 5 for corner sp, sp. Continue thus around, ending with 2 bls, join. Follow chart for remainder of pattern, always making an extra ch-5 at corners and working into center st of this ch on following rnd.

Make necessary number of motifs and sew together on wrong side with neat over-and-over stitches.

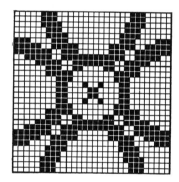

FRINGE... Make fringe in every other sp around. Cut 8 strands of thread, each 12 inches long. Double these strands, forming a loop. Pull loop through sp and draw loose ends through. Pull tight. When fringe has been worked all around edges, trim evenly to 4 inches.

Starbright

Continued from page 35

Continued from page 35

Join. **5th rnd:** Ch 3, dc in next 2 dc, * 3 dc in next loop, ch 6, 3 dc in next loop, dc in next 3 dc. Repeat from * around, ending with 3 dc in last loop. Join. **6th rnd:** Ch 3, dc in next 5 dc, * ch 7, dc in next 9 dc. Repeat from * around. Join. **7th rnd:** Ch 3, dc in next 5 dc, * ch 6, sc under next two chains, ch 6, dc in next 9 dc. Repeat from * around. Join. **8th rnd:** Ch 3, dc in next 2 dc, * (ch 6, sc in next loop) twice; ch 6, skip 3 dc, dc in next 3 dc. Repeat from * around. Join. **9th rnd:** Ch 3, dc in next 2 dc, * (ch 6, sc in next loop) 3 times; ch 6, dc in next 3 dc. Repeat from * around. Join. **10th rnd:** Ch 3, dc in next 2 dc, * (ch 7, sc in next loop) 4 times; ch 7, dc in next 3 dc. Repeat from * around. Join and break off.

SECOND BLOCK ... Work as for First Block until the 9th rnd is completed. **10th rnd:** Ch 3, dc in next 2 dc, ch 3, sl st in corresponding loop on First Block, ch 3, sc in next loop on Second Block and complete rnd as for First Block, joining next 4 loops as previous loop was joined.

For Single Size Spread, make 10 rows of 23 blocks and 9 rows of 24 blocks. For Double Size Spread, make 12 rows of 23 blocks and 11 rows of 24 blocks. Join blocks, alternating rows of 23 and 24 blocks (see diagram, page 14).

EDGING ... Attach thread to any loop on outer edge, sc in same loop, * ch 7, sc in next loop. Repeat from * around. Join and break off.

FRINGE . . . See above, having 15 strands, each 10 inches long.

MATERIALS:

CLARK'S O.N.T. MERCERIZED BEDSPREAD COTTON

SINGLE SIZE
42 balls of White or Ecru.

DOUBLE SIZE
56 balls of White or Ecru.

OR

J. & P. COATS KNIT-CRO-SHEEN

SINGLE SIZE
42 balls of White or Ecru,
or 68 balls of any color.

DOUBLE SIZE
56 balls of White or Ecru,
or 81 balls of any color.

Steel crochet hook No. 6.

GAUGE: Each motif measures about 7 inches from edge to edge, and 7¾ inches from point to point, before blocking. For a single size spread about 70 x 102 inches, make 161 motifs. For a double size spread about 91 x 102 inches, make 212 motifs.

Chevy Chase

FIRST MOTIF . . . Starting at center, ch 8. Join with sl st. **1st rnd:** Ch 3, 23 dc in ring. Join with sl st in top of 1st ch-3. **2nd rnd:** Ch 3, 4 dc in same place as sl st, drop loop from hook, insert hook in top st of ch-3 and pull loop through (a starting pc st), * ch 2, skip 1 dc, dc in next dc, ch 2, skip 1 dc, in next dc make 5 dc, drop loop from hook, insert hook in top of the 1st dc of this group and pull loop through (pc st). Repeat from * around. Join in top of 1st pc st. **3rd rnd:** Ch 3, starting pc st in top of 1st pc st, * ch 3, dc in next dc, ch 3, pc st in top of next pc st. Repeat from * around. Join. **4th rnd:** Ch 3, 4 dc in top of pc st, * ch 2, dc in next dc, ch 2, 5 dc in top of next pc st. Repeat from * around. Join. **5th rnd:** Ch 5, (dc in next dc, ch 2) 4 times; * in next dc make dc, ch 3 and dc; (ch 2, dc in next dc) 5 times; ch 2. Repeat from * around. Join with sl st in 3rd st of 1st ch-5. **6th rnd:** Sl st in next sp, ch 3, starting pc st in same sp, (ch 2, pc st in next sp) 3 times; ch 2, * in next ch-3 sp make dc, ch 3 and dc; ch 2, skip 1 sp, (pc st in next sp, ch 2) 4 times. Repeat from * around. Join.

7th rnd: Ch 3, starting pc st in top of 1st pc st, * (ch 2, pc st in next sp) 3 times; ch 2, pc st in top of next pc st, ch 2, in next ch-3 sp make dc, ch 3 and dc; ch 2, pc st in top of next pc st. Repeat from * around. Join. **8th rnd:** Ch 3, starting pc st in top of 1st pc st, * (ch 2, pc st in next sp) 4 times; ch 2, pc st in top of next pc st, ch 2, in next ch-3 sp make dc, ch 3 and dc; ch 2, pc st in top of next pc st. Repeat from * around. Join. **9th rnd:** Ch 3, starting pc st in top of 1st pc st, * (ch 2, pc st in next sp) 5 times; ch 2, pc st in top of next pc st, ch 2, in next ch-3 sp make dc, ch 3 and dc; ch 2, pc st in top of next pc st. Repeat from * around. Join. **10th rnd:** Sl st to next sp, ch 3, starting pc st in same sp, * (ch 4, sc in next sp, ch 4,

pc st in next sp, ch 2, pc st in next sp) twice; ch 2, in next ch-3 sp make dc, ch 3 and dc; (ch 2, pc st in next sp) twice. Repeat from * around, joining last ch-2 to top of 1st pc st. **11th rnd:** Ch 6, * (sc in next loop, ch 4) twice; pc st in next sp, (ch 4, sc in next loop) twice; ch 4, (pc st in next sp, ch 2) twice; in next ch-3 sp make dc, ch 3 and dc; (ch 2, pc st in next sp) twice; ch 4. Repeat from * around. Join to 3rd st of 1st ch-6. **12th rnd:** Sl st in next loop, ch 1, sc in same loop, (ch 4, sc in next loop) 6 times; * ch 4, pc st in next sp, ch 4, sc in next ch-3 sp, ch 4, pc st in next sp, (ch 4, sc in next loop) 8 times. Repeat from * around. Join with sl st to 1st sc made. **13th rnd:** Sl st to center of next loop, ch 1, sc in same loop, * ch 5, sc in next loop. Repeat from * around. Join and fasten off.

SECOND MOTIF . . . Work as for 1st motif until 12th rnd is completed. **13th rnd:** Sl st to center of next loop, ch 1, sc in same loop, (ch 5, sc in next loop) 9 times; (ch 2, sl st in corresponding loop on 1st motif, ch 2, sc in next loop on 2nd motif) 8 times; ch 5, sc in next loop on 2nd motif. Finish 2nd motif with no more joinings. Fasten off.

Make necessary number of motifs and join them as in diagram for joining hexagon motifs on page 31. For single size bedspread make 17 motifs from A to B, and 9 motifs from A to C; for double size spread, 17 motifs from A to B, and 12 motifs from A to C.

FRINGE . . . Make fringe in every other loop between scallops on both long sides as follows: Cut 20 strands, each 9 inches long. Double these strands forming a loop. Pull loop through 1st space and draw loose ends through loop. Pull tight (there should be 7 groups of fringe between scallops). Trim evenly.

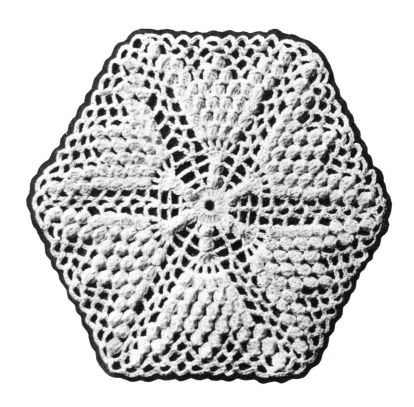

Marguerite

MATERIALS:

CLARK'S O.N.T. MERCERIZED BED-SPREAD COTTON: **Single Size Spread**—*68 x 104 inches*—*87 balls of White, Ecru or Cream, or 124 balls of Bed-spread Yellow*. **Double Size Spread**—*90 x 104 inches*—*108 balls of White, Ecru or Cream, or 155 balls of Bed-spread Yellow*.

STEEL CROCHET HOOK *No. 7*.

GAUGE: Block measures 12½ inches from side to side.

BLOCK . . . Starting at center, ch 9. Join with sl st. **1st rnd:** Ch 1, 18 sc in ring. Sl st in first sc. **2nd rnd:** Ch 3, 4 dc in back loop of next st, drop loop from hook, insert hook in top st of ch-3 and draw dropped loop through (pc st made), * ch 2, skip 1 sc, 5 dc in back loop of next sc, drop loop from hook, insert hook in first dc of 5-dc group and draw dropped loop through (another pc st made). Repeat from * around, ending with ch 2, sl st in top of first pc st. **3rd rnd:** Ch 5, * dc in next sp, ch 2, dc in top of next pc st, ch 2. Repeat from * around. Sl st in 3rd ch of ch-5. **4th rnd:** Ch 1, 3 sc in same place as sl st, * sc in next sp, 3 sc in next dc. Repeat from * around. Join with sl st to first sc.

Hereafter pick up only the back loop of each sc.

5th to 16th rnds incl: * 3 sc in next sc (center sc of 3-sc group), sc in each sc to center sc of next 3-sc group. Repeat from * around. Join (each 3-sc-group is the beginning of a petal—18 petals in rnd). **17th rnd:** Mark the center stitch between each petal with a colored thread. Then sl st in each sc to within 5 sc of first marker. * Holding the marker in left hand, fold the next petal back to 5 sts from marker, having right sides together. Then, working through both thicknesses, make sc in next 5 sts, ch 4. Repeat from * around, ending with ch 4. Join. **18th rnd:** Working in back loop only, make * sc in next 2 sc, 3 sc in next sc, sc in next 2 sc, sc in next 4 ch, (sc in next 5 sc, sc in next 4 ch) twice. Repeat from * around. Join. **19th to 23rd rnds incl:** Sc in each sc around, making 3 sc in center sc of each 3-sc group and ending with sl st in center sc of first 3-sc group. **24th rnd:** Ch 4, dc in same place as sl st, * (ch 1, skip 1 sc, dc in next sc) 18 times; ch 1, in center sc of next 3-sc group make dc, ch 1 and dc. Repeat from * around, ending with ch 1, sl st in 3rd st of ch-4 (120 sps in rnd). **25th rnd:** Sl st in sp, ch 4, dc in same sp, * (ch 1, dc in next sp) 19 times; ch 1, in next sp make dc, ch 1 and dc. Repeat from * around. Join (126 sps in rnd). **26th rnd:** * 3 sc in next st, sc in next 41 sts. Repeat from * around. Join (264 sc in rnd). **27th rnd:** Sl st in each st to center sc of first 3-sc group, * 3 sc in center sc, sc in next 3 sc, (pc st in next sc, sc in next 5 sc) 6 times; pc st in next sc, sc in next 3 sc. Repeat from * around. Join. **28th rnd:** 3 sc in next sc, sc in each st around, making 3 sc in center sc of each 3-sc group. Join. **29th rnd:** * 3 sc in center sc, sc in next 2 sc, (pc st in next sc, sc in next 5 sc) 7 times; pc st in next sc, sc in next 2 sc. Repeat from * around. Join.

30th rnd: Repeat 28th rnd. **31st rnd:** Sl st in center sc, ch 4, dc in same place as sl st, * (ch 1, skip 1 sc, dc in next sc) 25 times; ch 1, in center sc of next 3-sc group make dc, ch 1 and dc. Repeat from * around. Join. **32nd rnd:** Sl st in next sp, ch 4, dc in same sp, * (ch 1, dc in next sp) 26 times; ch 1, in next sp make dc, ch 1 and dc. Repeat from * around. Join. **33rd rnd:** * 3 sc in next st, sc in next 55 sts. Repeat from * around. Join. **34th rnd:** * 3 sc in center sc of 3-sc group, sc in next 4 sc, (pc st in next sc, sc in next 5 sc) 8 times; pc st in next sc, sc in next 4 sc. Repeat from * around. Join. **35th rnd:** * 3 sc in center sc, sc in each st to within center sc of next 3-sc group. Repeat from * around. Join. **36th rnd:** * 3 sc in next sc, sc in next 3 sc, (pc st in next sc, sc in next 5 sc) 9 times; pc st in next sc, sc in next 3 sc. Repeat from * around. Join. **37th rnd:** Repeat 35th rnd. **38th rnd:** * 3 sc in center sc, sc in next 2 sc, (pc st in next sc, sc in next 5 sc) 10 times; pc st in next sc, sc in next 2 sc. Repeat from * around. Join. **39th rnd:** Repeat 35th rnd. **40th rnd:** Sl st in center sc, ch 4, dc in same place, * (ch 1, skip 1 sc, dc in next sc) 34 times; ch 1, in center sc of next 3-sc group make dc, ch 1 and dc. Repeat from * around. Join. **41st rnd:** Sl st in sp, ch 4, dc in same sp, * (ch 1, dc in next sp) 35 times; ch 1, in next sp make dc, ch 1 and dc. Repeat from * around. Join and break off.

HALF BLOCK . . . Starting at center, ch 9. Join with sl st. **1st row:** 9 sc in ring, sl st in last 3 ch of ring, sl st in first sc. **2nd row:** Ch 3, 4 dc in same place as sl st and complete pc st as before, (ch 2, skip 1 sc, make a 5-dc pc st in back loop of next sc) 4 times. Break off.

Note: Hereafter, break off at end of each row and attach thread to beginning of previous row.

40

3rd row: Attach thread to tip of first pc st, ch 5, * dc in next sp, ch 2, dc in next pc st, ch 2. Repeat from * across, ending with ch 2, dc in tip of last pc st (8 sps). Break off. **4th row:** Attach thread to 3rd ch of ch-5, * sc in sp, 3 sc in next dc. Repeat from * across, ending with 3 sc in last dc. Break off. **Hereafter pick up only the back loop of each st. 5th to 16th rows incl:** Sc in each sc across, making 3 sc in center sc of each 3-sc group. Break off. **17th row:** Mark the center st between each petal with a colored thread. Place a pin in 9th sc from beginning of previous row. With wrong side facing attach thread to sc at pin, ch 5, skip 3 sc, sc in next 5 sc. Turn work so that right side is facing, * ch 5, holding the marker in left hand, fold the next petal back to 5 sts from marker, then, working through both thicknesses, make sc in next 5 sts. Repeat from * 6 more times; then with wrong side of last petal facing make sc in last 5 sc (85 sts on row). Break off. **18th row:** Attach

thread to first ch and make sc in each st across (85 sc). Break off. **19th row:** Attach thread to first sc, 2 sc in same place, (sc in next 27 sc, 3 sc in next sc) twice; sc in next 27 sc, 2 sc in last sc. Break off. **20th to 23rd rows incl:** Sc in each sc across, making 2 sc in first and last sc and 3 sc in center sc of each 3-sc group (115 sc on 23rd row). **24th row:** Attach thread to first sc, ch 4, dc in same place, * (ch 1, skip 1 sc, dc in next sc) 18 times; ch 1, in center dc of next 3-sc group make dc, ch 1 and dc. Repeat from * across, ending with dc, ch 1 and dc in last sc. Break off.

Hereafter work as for Block to within last 2 rows, always making an extra sp at beginning and end of each row of sps and 2 sc at beginning and end of each sc-row (214 sc on last row). Now work 2 rnds all around as follows: **1st rnd:** Attach thread to first sc, ch 4, dc in same sp, * (ch 1, skip 1 sc, dc in next sc) 34 times; ch 1, in center st of next 3-sc group make dc, ch 1

and dc. Repeat from * across 3 sides, ending with dc, ch 1 and dc in last sc. Continue making ch-1 sps along remaining side, ending with ch 1, sl st in 3rd ch of ch-4. **2nd rnd:** Sl st in sp, ch 4, dc in same sp, * ch 1, dc in next sp. Repeat from * around, making dc, ch 1 and dc in each corner sp. Join and break off.

For Single Size Spread, make 3 rows of 8 blocks and 2 rows of 7 blocks. For Double Size Spread, make 4 rows of 8 blocks and 3 rows of 7 blocks. Sew blocks neatly together on wrong side. Fill in spaces at top and bottom of spread with half blocks.

FRINGE . . . Cut 10 strands of thread, each 12 inches long. Double these strands to form a loop. Insert hook in space on edge of bedspread and draw loop through. Draw loose ends through loop and pull up tightly to form a knot. Make a fringe in every other space (or every half inch) around spread. When fringe is completed, trim ends evenly.

Popcorn Pinwheel

MATERIALS: J. & P. Coats Bedspread Cotton, *24 balls of White or Ecru for single size spread; 30 balls for double size spread.*
Milward's *steel crochet hook No. 8 or 9.*

GAUGE: Each motif measures about 6 inches across, from side to side. For a single size spread, about 72 x 110 inches including fringe, make 214 motifs. For a double size spread, about 92 x 110 inches including fringe, make 280 motifs.

MOTIF... Starting at center, ch 12, join with sl st.
1st rnd: Ch 3, 23 d c in ring. Join to 3rd st of ch-3.
2nd rnd: Ch 3, 4 d c in same place as sl st; drop st from hook, insert hook back in 3rd st of ch-3 first made and draw loop through the one on hook (a pc st). * Ch 5, skip 2 d c, d c in next d c, ch 3, 5 d c in next d c; drop st from hook, insert hook back in last ch made and draw loop through the one on hook (a pc st). Repeat from * around, ending with ch 2, sl st at tip of first pc st made. **3rd rnd:** Sl st in ch-5 sp, ch 3 and complete a pc st; * ch 2, a pc st, ch 5, d c in next sp, ch 2, a pc st. Repeat from * around, ending with ch 2, sl st at tip of 1st pc st made. **4th rnd:** Sl st in next sp (between pc sts), ch 3 and complete a pc st; * ch 2, in next ch-5 sp make 2 pc sts with ch-2 between; ch 5, d c in next sp, ch 2, pc st in sp between 2 pc sts. Repeat from * around, ending as before. **5th and 6th rnds:** Same as 4th rnd, making pc sts between pc sts of previous rnd and 2 pc sts in ch-5 sp, always making ch-2 between pc sts (4 pc sts in each group on 5th rnd; 5 pc sts in each group on 6th rnd). **7th rnd:** Sl st in next sp (between 1st 2 pc sts), ch 3 and complete a pc st; * (ch 2, pc st between next 2 pc sts) 3 times; ch 3, d c at tip of next pc st, ch 3, d c in ch-5 sp, ch 3, d c in next sp, ch 2, pc st between next 2 pc sts. Repeat from * around. Join. **8th rnd:** * 3 pc sts between pc sts of previous rnd, with ch-2 between; ch 3, d c at tip of next pc st; (ch 3, d c in next sp) 4 times; ch 2 and repeat from * around. Join. **9th rnd:** * 2 pc sts between pc sts of previous rnd, with ch-2 between; ch 3, d c at tip of next pc st; (ch 3, d c in next sp) 6 times, ch 2. Repeat from * around. Join. **10th rnd:** Sl st in sp (between pc sts), ch 3 and complete a pc st; * (ch 3, d c in next sp) 3 times; ch 3, skip next d c and sp; in next d c make 3 tr, ch 3, 3 tr; ch 3, skip next sp and d c; d c in next sp; (ch 3, d c in next sp) twice, ch 2, pc st between pc sts of previous rnd. Repeat from * around. Join and fasten off.

Make necessary number of motifs and sew together on wrong side with neat over-and-over stitches, as in diagram on page 29 (for single size spread, disregard motifs to left of heavy line).

FRINGE... Make fringe in each sp around four sides as follows: Cut 8 strands, each 12 inches long. Double these strands, forming a loop. Pull loop through sp and draw loose ends through loop. Pull tight. When fringe has been worked around all edges, trim evenly.

SINGLE SIZE

Filet Medallion Bedspread

MATERIALS:

J. & P. COATS KNIT-CRO-SHEEN

SINGLE SIZE
26 balls of White or Ecru,
or 42 balls of any color.

DOUBLE SIZE
37 balls of White or Ecru,
or 59 balls of any color.

OR

CLARK'S O.N.T. MERCERIZED BEDSPREAD COTTON

SINGLE SIZE
26 balls of White or Ecru.

DOUBLE SIZE
37 balls of White or Ecru.

Steel crochet hook No. 7 or 8.

GAUGE: 3 sps make 1¼ inches; 3 rnds make 1¼ inches. Each block measures about 17½ inches after blocking. For a single size spread about 72 x 108 inches including edging, make 4 x 6 blocks. For a double size spread about 90 x 108 inches including edging, make 5 x 6 blocks.

DIRECTIONS ON PAGE 46.

Cameo

This lovely spellbinder with its central garland of
roses, its border and pillow motif, its clusters of popcorns, makes
a charming picture. Clear-cut as a cameo and just as precious.

DIRECTIONS ON PAGE 46.

Filet Medallion Bedspread

ILLUSTRATED ON PAGE 44.

BLOCK . . . Starting at center, ch 11, join with sl st to form ring. **1st rnd:** Ch 4 (to count as tr), 4 tr in ring, (ch 7, 5 tr in ring) 3 times; ch 7. Join with sl st to top of ch-4. **2nd rnd:** Ch 4, tr in next 4 tr, * 4 tr in next sp, ch 7, 4 tr in same sp, tr in next 5 tr. Repeat from * around. Join. **3rd rnd:** Ch 4, tr in 8 tr, * 4 tr in next sp, ch 7, 4 tr in same sp, tr in next 13 tr. Repeat from * around. Join. **4th rnd:** Ch 4, tr in 4 tr, * (ch 3, skip 3 tr, tr in next tr) twice; in corner sp make 4 tr, ch 7 and 4 tr; tr in next tr, (ch 3, skip 3 tr, tr in next tr) twice; tr in next 4 tr. Repeat from * around. Join. **5th rnd:** Ch 4, tr in 4 tr, * ch 3, tr in next tr, 3 tr in next sp, tr in next 5 tr, in corner sp make

4 tr, ch 7 and 4 tr, tr in 5 tr, 3 tr in next sp, tr in next tr, ch 3, tr in next tr, tr in next 4 tr. Repeat from * around. Join. **6th to 20th rnds incl:** Work in this manner following chart, making ch-3 for sps and ch-7 for corner sps, and joining each rnd with a sl st. The heavy line on chart shows where each rnd begins. At end of 20th rnd, join and fasten off. Make necessary number of blocks and sew together on wrong side with neat over-and-over sts.

EDGING . . . Attach thread, ch 4 and work 3 rnds of tr making corners as on blocks, being careful edging does not ruffle. Fasten off. Block to measurements given.

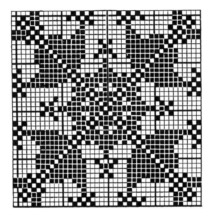

There are 10 spaces
between heavy lines

Cameo

ILLUSTRATED ON PAGE 45.

For Double Size Bed Only

MATERIALS:
J. & P. COATS BEDSPREAD COTTON
24 balls of White or Ecru

MILWARD'S STEEL CROCHET HOOK No. 7 or 8.

GAUGE:

4 sps or bls make 1 inch; 4 rows make 1 inch. Finished bedspread measures about 90 x 108 inches after blocking.

Starting at bottom of Chart One, make a chain (12 ch sts to 1 inch) about 3 yards long. **1st row:** D c in 8th ch from hook, * ch 2, skip 2 ch, d c in next ch. Repeat from * until there are 359 sps made. Cut off remaining chain (mark the 180th sp with a colored thread—this is center). Ch 5, turn. **2nd row:** (This is right side) D c in next d c (sp over sp), 11 more sps, * make a pc st in next sp—*to make a pc st, ch 1, 5 d c in sp, drop loop from hook, insert hook in ch-1, and draw dropped loop through;* d c in next d c. Repeat from * 8 more times; 11 sps, (5 pc sts, 7 sps) 11 times; (5 pc sts, 8 sps)

twice, (5 pc sts, 7 sps) 11 times; 5 pc sts, 11 sps, 9 pc sts, 12 sps. Ch 5, turn. **3rd row:** Make 10 sps, (make a reverse pc st in next sp—*to make a reverse pc st, work as for pc st, only inserting hook in ch-1 from back of work, thus raising pc st to right side;* d c in next d c) twice; 9 sps, 3 reverse pc sts, 7 sps, (1 reverse pc st, 5 sps) 24 times; 2 reverse pc sts, 5 sps, 2 reverse pc sts, (5 sps, 1 reverse pc st) 24 times; 7 sps, 3 reverse pc sts, 9 sps, 2 reverse pc sts, 10 sps. Ch 5, turn.

Now follow chart, starting at 4th row, always working to center of row as on chart (chart shows only the first half of each row); then omitting the center sp or pc st-bl, as the case may be, follow chart back to the beginning of row. When 24th row has been completed, work as follows: Ch 5, turn. **25th row:** 2 sps, 1 pc st, 2 sps, 5 pc sts, 9 sps, 1 pc st, 28 sps, make a bl over next sp—*to make a bl, make 2 d c in sp, d c in next d c;* 11 sps, 1 bl, 25 sps, 16 sps, 3 bls, 21 sps, 1 bl, 20 sps, 1 bl, 19 sps, 6 bls, 11 sps, 6 bls, 19 sps, 1 bl, 20 sps, 1 bl, 21 sps, 3 bls, 16 sps, 1 bl, 25 sps, 1 bl, 11 sps, 1 bl, 28 sps, 1 pc st, 9 sps, 5 pc sts, 2 sps, 1 pc st, 2 sps. Ch 5, turn.

Starting with 26th row, follow chart to top. Reverse chart and omitting last row, work back to "A" (this last row completes center design). *Floral Borders* are now worked from "B" toward top of chart; at the same time, keep continuity of popcorn all-over pattern and popcorn scallop design along edges until the 324th row is complete. **Next row:** Mark off the center 119 sps. Continue bedspread as before, following Chart Two when working across the center 119 sps. Continue thus, until top of Chart Two is reached. Work scallop design, floral borders and all-over pattern as before, until 408 rows are complete. Do not fasten off but work s c all around, keeping work flat. Fasten off. Block to measure 90 x 108 inches.

Cameo

CENTER OF WIDTH   CHART TWO

THERE ARE 10 SPACES
BETWEEN HEAVY LINES

CENTER OF WIDTH   ◨ POPCORN-PC ST.   □ SPACE-SP.   ■ BLOCK-BL   CHART ONE

Textured Beauty

MATERIALS—Lily FROST-TONE Mercerized Crochet Cotton:—Single Bed Size—11x18 Blocks—74x107 inches, including fringe—32 cones of White, Cream or Ecru. Double Bed Size—14x18 Blocks—90x107 inches, including fringe—41 cones.

Crochet hook size 10.

BLOCK—(Size—5½ inches when blocked)—Ch 9, sl st in starting st. Ch 1, 2 sc in ring. Now make a puff—Ch 7, 7 dtr in 7th ch st from hook, holding back the last lp of each dtr on hook, thread over and pull thru all 8 lps on hook at once (a Cluster), ch 4, sl st in lp at top of Cluster for a p, ch 7, sl st at base of Cluster in same st where dtr were worked (1 puff made). This will not be mentioned again. (3 sc in ring, a puff) 3 times, 1 sc in ring, sl st in 1st sc. **ROW 2**—Ch 3 and holding puffs down in front, make * dc in next sc, sk puff, dc in next sc, ** (dc, ch 5, dc) in next sc. Repeat from * twice and from * to **. Dc in next st, ch 2, dc in top of 1st 3-ch. **ROW 3**—Ch 3, turn, 2 dc in next 2-ch sp, * dc in next 4 dc, ** (3 dc, ch 5, 3 dc) in corner sp. Repeat from * twice and from * to **. 3 dc in next sp, ch 2, dc in top of 1st 3-ch. **ROW 4**—Ch 3, turn, 2 dc in next 2-ch, * dc in next 4 dc, sl st in p at tip of puff, ch 1, sk 2 dc behind puff, dc in next 4 dc, ** (3 dc, ch 5, 3 dc) in corner sp. Repeat from * twice and from * to **. 3 dc in next sp, ch 2, dc in top of 1st 3-ch. **ROW 5**—Ch 5, turn, dc in next dc, * (ch 2, dc in next 3d st) 5 times, ** ch 2, (dc, ch 5, dc) in 3d st of corner 5-ch, ch 2, dc in next dc. Repeat from * twice and from * to **. (Ch 2, dc in next 3d st) twice. **ROW 6**—Ch 1, turn, (2 sc, a puff and 1 sc) in next sp, * sc in next dc, 2 sc in next sp, sc in dc, (sc, a puff, sc) in next sp. Repeat from * twice. Sc in dc, 2 sc in next sp, sc in dc, (1 sc, a puff, 3 sc, a puff and 1 sc) in corner sp. Repeat from * around. In final sp, make 1 sc, a puff and 1 sc, sl st in 1st sc. **ROW 7**—Ch 5, * (sk 1 sc on each side of puff, dc in next 4 sc, ch 2) 4 times, (dc, ch 5, dc) in corner sc, ch 2. Repeat from * around. Sk 1 sc on each side of final puff, dc in next st, ch 2, dc in 3d st of 1st 5-ch. **ROW 8**—Ch 3, turn, 2 dc in 2-ch sp, * dc in next dc, (ch 2, dc in next 4 dc) 4 times, ch 2, dc in next dc, ** (3 dc, ch 5, 3 dc) in corner sp. Repeat from * twice and from * to **. 3 dc in next sp, ch 2, dc in top of 1st 3-ch. **ROW 9**—Ch 3, turn, 2 dc in 2-ch sp, * dc in next 4 dc, (sl st in p at top of next Cluster, ch 1, dc in next 4 dc) 5 times, ** (3 dc, ch 4, 3 dc) in corner sp. Repeat from * twice and from * to **. 3 dc in next sp, dc in top of 1st 3-ch. **Corner**—Ch 4, turn, sk last 4 dc, * dc in next dc, (ch 2, dc in next 3d st) twice, ch 9, sk 9 sts, sc in next 2 sts, ch 9, sk 9 sts, dc in next dc, (ch 2, dc in next 3d st) twice, dc in next 3d dc. **ROW 2**—Ch 4, turn, sk last 2 dc, dc in next dc, 2 dc in next sp, dc in dc, ch 2, dc in next 3d ch st, ch 7, sc in next 2 sc, ch 7, dc in next 7th ch st, ch 2, dc in next dc, 2 dc in next sp, dc in next 2 dc. **ROW 3**—Ch 4, turn, sk last 4 dc, dc in next dc, 2 dc in next sp, dc in dc, 3 dc in next sp, ch 6, sc in 2 center sc, ch 6, 3 dc on left end of next 7-ch, dc in next dc, 2 dc in next sp, dc in next dc, dc in next 3d dc. **ROW 4**—Ch 4, turn, sk last 4 dc, dc in next 4 dc, ch 3, dtr in 2 center sc, ch 3, dc in next 4 dc, dc in next 3d dc. **ROW 5**—Ch 4, turn, sk last 4 dc, dc in next dc, 3 dc in next sp, ch 2, 3 dc in next sp, dc in next dc, dc in next 3d dc. **ROW 6**—

Ch 4, turn, sk last 4 dc, dc in next dc, 2 dc in next sp, dc in next dc, dc in next 3d dc. Ch 5, turn, sk last 4 dc, sl st in next dc. Cut 2 inches long and pull thru lp tightly. Sk next 7 sps down side, join to next dc, ch 4, sk 2 dc and repeat corner from *. Continue until 4 corners are completed. **Edge**—Joining to one corner of Block, * make 3 sc in corner sp, ch 4, sl st in last sc for a p, 3 sc in same sp, (2 sc, a p and 2 sc in next sp) 13 times, working over end left from corner. Repeat from * around and join. Cut 6 inches long, thread to a needle and fasten off on back.

Make and join Blocks to desired size by the p at corners and by the 13 ps on each side. To join, in place of a p, make 2-ch, sl st in corresponding p on 1st Block, ch 2, sl st back in last sc to complete p. Repeat with each p-joining.

EDGE—Join to one corner, ch 4, sc in same p, * ch 4, sc in next 3d sc, (ch 4, sc in next p) 13 times, ch 4, sc in next 3d sc, ch 4, sc in joining of Blocks. Repeat from * around, making an extra lp at each corner. Fasten off.

FRINGE—Cut a stiff cardboard 8 inches long. Wind thread 8 times around card and cut at one end. Double these 16-inch strands to form a lp. Insert hook up from underneath thru a 4-ch sp on Edge, catch lp and pull thru, pass ends thru lp and pull tight. Repeat in each sp around both sides and bottom of Spread. Then knot tog. 8 strands of 2 adjacent knots, ½ inch down from 1st row of knots. Continue thus along entire fringe. Comb out fringe and trim evenly.

Stretch and pin Spread right-side-down in true shape on a padded board or table, or on curtain or quilting frames. Steam and press dry thru a cloth. If stretched on frames, lay over an ironing board, and steam and press dry in sections until completed.

Berkeley Square

The classic square motif with its placid dignity has a
stately air that is at home in both modern and traditional settings.

MATERIALS:
CLARK'S O.N.T. OR J. & P. COATS
BIG BALL BEST SIX CORD MERCERIZED CROCHET, in size 20

SINGLE SIZE
65 balls of White or Ecru.

DOUBLE SIZE
81 balls of White or Ecru.

MILWARD'S STEEL CROCHET HOOK No. 8 or 9.

GAUGE:
Each block measures about 6 inches square before blocking. For a single size spread,
about 74 x 110 inches, make 12 x 18 blocks. For a double size spread, about 92 x 110
inches, make 15 x 18 blocks.

BLOCK ... Starting at center, ch 16, join with sl st to form ring. **1st rnd:** Ch 3, 31 d c in ring. Join to 3rd st of ch-3. **2nd rnd:** Ch 6, * skip 1 d c, d c in next d c, ch 3. Repeat from * around. Join to 3rd st of ch-6 (16 sps). **3rd rnd:** Into each ch-3 sp make s c, half d c, 3 d c, half d c and s c (a petal). **4th rnd:** Sl st in each st to 2nd d c of 1st petal incl., ch 11, tr tr in same place as sl st; * (ch 4, d c in 2nd d c of next petal) 3 times; ch 4, into 2nd d c of next petal make tr tr, ch 5 and tr tr. Repeat from * around. Join last ch-4 with sl st to 6th ch of ch-11 first made. **5th rnd:** * Into corner loop make 4 s c, ch 1 and 4 s c; 5 s c in each of next 4 loops. Repeat from * around; join. **6th and 7th rnds:** S c in each s c around, making s c, ch 1 and s c in each corner; join. **8th rnd:** Sl st to ch-1 incl. at corner, ch 8, d c in same place as sl st; * (ch 3, skip 2 s c, d c in next s c) 10 times; ch 3; into corner ch-1 make d c, ch 5 and d c. Repeat from * around, ending with ch 3, sl st in 3rd st of ch-8.

9th rnd: Sl st in loop, ch 3; in corner loop make d c, 2 tr, ch 3, 2 tr and 2 d c; * s c in next sp; (into next sp make 2 d c, tr, ch 3, tr and 2 d c; s c in next sp) 5 times; in corner loop make 2 d c, 2 tr, ch 3, 2 tr and 2 d c. Repeat from * around; join. **10th rnd:** Sl st in each st to within corner ch-3 loop, sl st in 1st st of ch-3, s c in loop, * ch 7, s c in next loop (between tr); then (ch 6, s c in next loop) 4 times; ch 7, s c in corner loop. Repeat from * around; join. **11th rnd:** Ch 2 (to count as s c and ch-1), s c in same place as sl st, * 6 s c in next loop, s c in next s c; (7 s c in next loop, s c in next s c) 4 times; 7 s c in next loop, in corner s c make s c, ch 1 and s c. Repeat from * around; join. **12th, 13th and 14th rnds:** S c in each s c around, making s c, ch 1 and s c in each corner. **15th rnd:** Sl st in each st to ch-1 at corner incl., ch 3, d c in same place as sl st, ch 3, 2 d c in same place. * (Ch 2, skip 2 s c, d c in next 2 d c) 13 times; ch 2, into corner ch-1 make 2 d c, ch 3 and 2 d c. Repeat from * around; join. **16th rnd:** Sl st in next d c and in corner sp, ch 3, d c in same place as last sl st, ch 3, 2 d c in same place; * (ch 2, 2 d c in next sp) 14 times; ch 2, into corner ch-3 sp make 2 d c, ch 3 and 2 d c. Repeat from * around; join.

17th rnd: Sl st in next d c and in corner sp; ch 3, make d c, ch 3 and 2 d c in same place as last sl st. * (Ch 2, 2 d c in next sp) 4 times; (d c in next 2 d c, 2 d c in next sp) 8 times; (ch 2, 2 d c in next sp) 3 times; ch 2, into corner ch-3 make 2 d c, ch 3 and 2 d c. Repeat from * around; join. **18th rnd:** Sl st in next d c and in corner sp, ch 3; make d c, ch 3 and 2 d c in same place as last sl st. * (Ch 2, 2 d c in next sp) 4 times; ch 2, skip 2 d c, d c in next 30 d c; (ch 2, 2 d c in next sp) 4 times; ch 2, into corner ch-3 make 2 d c, ch 3 and 2 d c. Repeat from * around; join. **19th rnd:** Sl st in next d c and in corner sp, ch 3; make d c, ch 3 and 2 d c in same place as last sl st. * (Ch 2, 2 d c in next sp) 5 times; ch 2, skip 2 d c, d c in next 26 d c; (ch 2, 2 d c in next sp) 5 times; ch 2, into corner ch-3 make 2 d c, ch 3 and 2 d c. Repeat from * around. Fasten off. This completes one block.

Make the necessary number of blocks and sew them together on wrong side with neat over-and-over stitches. Block to measurements given.

MATERIALS:

CLARK'S O.N.T. or J. & P. COATS
BEST SIX CORD MERCERIZED CROCHET, size 20:

SINGLE SIZE	DOUBLE SIZE
SMALL BALL:	SMALL BALL:
CLARK'S O.N.T.—99 balls,	CLARK'S O.N.T.—135 balls,
OR	OR
J. & P. COATS —57 balls.	J. & P. COATS —78 balls.
BIG BALL:	BIG BALL:
J. & P. COATS —33 balls.	J. & P. COATS —45 balls.

Steel crochet hook No. 8 or 9.

GAUGE: Each motif measures 1¼ inches square before blocking. For single size, spread about 72 x 108 inches including edging, make **15 x 24** motifs; for double size spread about 90 x 108 inches including edging, make **20 x 24** motifs.

Nocturne

FIRST MOTIF . . . Ch 7, join with sl st. **1st rnd:** Ch 4 (to count as 1 tr), 23 tr in ring. Join with sl st in top st of 1st ch-4. **2nd rnd:** Ch 4, tr in next 2 tr, * ch 5, tr in next 3 tr. Repeat from * around, joining last ch-5 to top st of 1st ch-4. **3rd rnd:** Sl st in next st, ch 4, tr in next tr, 3 tr in next loop, * ch 6, skip next tr, tr in next 2 tr, 3 tr in next loop. Repeat from * around. Join. **4th rnd:** Sl st in next st, ch 4, tr in next 3 tr, 3 tr in next loop, * ch 7, skip 1 tr, tr in next 4 tr, 3 tr in next loop. Repeat from * around. Join. **5th rnd:** Sl st in next st, ch 4, tr in next 5 tr, 3 tr in next loop, * ch 11, skip next tr, tr in next 6 tr, 3 tr in next loop. Repeat from * around. Join. **6th rnd:** Sl st in next st, ch 4, tr in next 4 tr, * ch 8, in center st of loop below make tr, ch 2, tr, ch 5, tr, ch 2 and tr; ch 8, skip 1 tr, tr in next 5 tr, ch 8, sc in next loop, ch 8, skip 1 tr, tr in next 5 tr. Repeat from * around. Join. **7th rnd:** Sl st in next st, ch 4, tr in next 2 tr, * ch 8, sc in next loop, ch 8, in next ch-5 sp (corner sp) make tr, ch 2, tr, ch 2 and tr; ch 8, sc in next loop, ch 8, skip next tr, tr in next 3 tr, ch 8, sc in next loop, ch 8, sc in next loop, ch 8, skip next tr, tr in next 3 tr. Repeat from * around. Join and fasten off.

SECOND MOTIF . . . Work 1st 6 rnds as for 1st motif. **7th rnd:** Sl st in next st, ch 4, tr in next 2 tr, ch 8, sc in next loop, ch 8, in next ch-5 sp make tr, ch 2 and tr; ch 3, sl st in corner sp on 1st motif, ch 3, in same sp on 2nd motif where last tr was made make tr, ch 2 and tr; ch 4, sl st in next loop on 1st motif, ch 4, sc in next loop on 2nd motif, ch 4, sl st in next loop on 1st motif, ch 4, skip next tr, tr in next 3 tr, (ch 4, sl st in next loop on 1st motif, ch 4, sc in next loop on 2nd motif) twice; ch 4, sl st in next loop on 1st motif, ch 4, skip next tr on 2nd motif, tr in next 3 tr,

ch 4, sl st in next loop on 1st motif, ch 4, sc in next loop on 2nd motif, ch 4, sl st in next loop on 1st motif, ch 4, in ch-5 sp on 2nd motif make tr, ch 2 and tr; ch 3, sl st to corner sp of 1st motif, ch 3, in same sp on 2nd motif where last tr was made, make tr, ch 2 and tr. Complete rnd as for 1st motif. Make necessary number of motifs, joining adjacent sides as 2nd motif was joined to 1st (wherever 4 corners meet, join 3rd and 4th corners to joining of other corners).

EDGING . . . Attach thread to 1st joining preceding a corner. Ch 1, sc in same place, (ch 10, sc in next loop) 7 times; ch 10, in corner sp make tr, ch 3, tr, ch 5, tr, ch 3 and tr; * (ch 10, sc in next loop) 7 times; ch 10, sc in joining of motifs. Repeat from * around, turning corners as 1st corner was turned and joining last ch-10 to 1st sc made. **2nd to 6th rnds incl:** Sl st to center of next loop, ch 1, sc in same loop, * ch 10, sc in next loop. Repeat from * around and continue turning corners as before. **7th rnd:** Sl st to center of next loop, ch 4, 2 tr in same loop, * ch 8, sc in next loop, ch 8, 3 tr in next loop. Repeat from * around, making 3 tr in corner sps and joining last ch-8 to 4th st of 1st ch-4. **8th rnd:** Sl st in next 2 sts, ch 4, 2 tr in next loop, ch 8, sc in same loop, * sc in next loop, ch 8, 2 tr in same loop, tr in next tr, ch 5, sc in 5th ch from hook (a p made), skip 1 tr, tr in next tr, 2 tr in next loop, ch 8, sc in same loop. Repeat from * 2 more times. For corner make sc in next loop, ch 8, 2 tr in next loop, in next tr make tr, p and tr; tr in next tr, in next tr make tr, p and tr; 2 tr in next loop, ch 8, sc in same loop; ** sc in next loop, ch 8, 2 tr in loop, tr in next tr, p, skip 1 tr, tr in next tr, 2 tr in next loop, ch 8, sc in same loop. Repeat from ** around, turning corners as 1st corner was turned. Join and fasten off.

53

Gracie Square

MATERIALS:

CLARK'S O.N.T. MERCERIZED BEDSPREAD COTTON

SINGLE SIZE
32 balls.

DOUBLE SIZE
39 balls.

Steel crochet hook No. 5.

GAUGE: Each block measures 4 inches square before blocking. For a single spread
72 x 105 inches, make 18 x 26 blocks; for a double spread 90 x 105 inches, make 22 x 26 blocks.

DIRECTIONS ON PAGE 56.

Prophecy

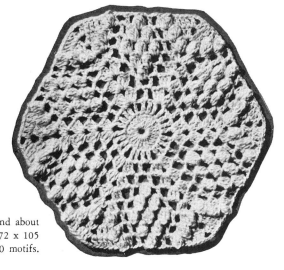

MATERIALS:

J. & P. COATS KNIT-CRO-SHEEN

SINGLE SIZE
50 balls of White or Ecru,
or 80 balls of **any** color.

DOUBLE SIZE
62 balls of White or Ecru,
or 98 balls of **any** color.

Steel crochet hook No. 7 or 8.

GAUGE: Each motif measures about 5¾ inches from point to opposite point, and about 5 inches from side to opposite side before blocking. For single size spread about 72 x 105 inches, make 348 motifs; for double size spread about 90 x 105 inches, make 430 motifs.

DIRECTIONS ON PAGE 56.

Gracie Square

ILLUSTRATED ON PAGE 54.

BLOCK . . . Starting at center ch 10. Join. **1st rnd:** Ch 1, * sc in ring, ch 5. Repeat from * 3 more times. **2nd rnd:** * Sc in next sc, 2 sc in next sp, ch 5. Repeat from * 3 more times. **3rd, 4th and 5th rnds:** * Sc in each sc around, 2 sc in sp, ch 5. Repeat from * 3 more times. **6th rnd:** Same as 5th rnd making ch 6 (instead of ch 5). **7th rnd:** * Skip next sc, sc in each sc around to within last sc of group, ch 6, sc in next loop, ch 6. Repeat from * 3 more times. **8th rnd:** * Skip next sc, sc in each sc around to within last sc of group, (ch 7, sc in next loop) twice; ch 7. Repeat from * 3 more times. **9th rnd:** * Skip next sc, sc in each sc around to within last sc of group, (ch 7, sc in next loop) 3 times; ch 7. Repeat from * 3 more times. **10th rnd:** * Skip next sc, sc in each sc around to within last sc of group, (ch 7, sc in next loop) 4 times; ch 7. Repeat from * around, ending with sc in last loop. **11th rnd:** Ch 8, dc in next loop, ch 5, dc in next loop, * ch 5, in center st of next loop make dc, ch 9 and dc; (ch 5, dc in next loop) 4 times. Repeat from * around. Join last ch-5 with sl st to 3rd st of ch-8. **12th rnd:** Ch 3, dc in each st around, making 3 dc in center st of each corner loop. Join and fasten off.

Make necessary number of blocks and sew them together on wrong side with neat over-and-over stitches. Block to measurements given.

Prophecy

ILLUSTRATED ON PAGE 55.

MOTIF . . . Starting at center, ch 10. Join with sl st. **1st rnd:** Ch 3 (to count as dc), 23 dc in ring. Join with sl st in top st of 1st ch-3. **2nd rnd:** Ch 4 (to count as dc and ch 1), * dc in next dc, ch 1. Repeat from * around. Join with sl st to 3rd st of ch-4. **3rd rnd:** Sl st in next sp, ch 3, in same sp make 2 dc, ch 3 and 3 dc (starting shell made) ; * ch 2, skip 1 sp, dc in next sp, ch 2, skip 1 sp, in next sp make 3 dc, ch 3 and 3 dc (another shell made). Repeat from * around. Join. **4th rnd:** Sl st in next 2 sts, sl st in next sp, ch 3, make starting shell in same sp; * (ch 2, dc in next sp) twice; ch 2, make a shell in sp of shell below. Repeat from * around. Join. **5th rnd:** Sl st in next 2 sts, sl st in next sp, ch 3, make starting shell in same sp; * ch 2, dc in next sp, ch 2, 5 dc in next sp, drop loop from hook, insert hook in top of 1st dc of this group and pull dropped loop through (pc st made) ; ch 2, dc in next sp, ch 2, make shell in sp of shell below. Repeat from * around. Join.

6th rnd: Sl st in next 2 sts, sl st in next sp, ch 3, make starting shell in same sp; * ch 2, dc in next sp, (ch 2, pc st in next sp) twice; ch 2, dc in next sp, ch 2, shell in sp of shell below. Repeat from * around. Join. **7th rnd:** Sl st in next dc, ch 3, pc st in top of next dc, in next sp make dc, ch 3 and dc; pc st in top of next dc, dc in next dc, * ch 2, dc in next sp, ch 2, (pc st in next sp, ch 2) 3 times; dc in next sp, ch 2, skip 1 dc, dc in next dc, pc st in top of next dc, in next sp make dc, ch 3 and dc; pc st in top of next dc, dc in next dc. Repeat from * around. Join. **8th rnd:** Ch 3, pc st in same place as sl st, dc in top of pc st below, dc in next dc, in next sp make dc, ch 3 and dc; dc in next dc, dc in top of pc st below, pc st in top of next dc, * (dc in next sp, ch 2) twice; (pc in next sp, ch 2) twice; dc in next sp, ch 2, dc in next sp, pc st in top of next dc, dc in top of pc st below, dc in next dc, in next sp make dc, ch 3 and dc; dc in next dc, dc in top of next pc st, pc st in

top of next dc. Repeat from * around, ending with dc in last sp. Join. **9th rnd:** Ch 3, dc in top of pc st, dc in next 2 dc, in next sp make dc, ch 3 and dc; dc in next 3 dc, dc in top of pc st, pc st in next dc, * (dc in next sp, ch 2) twice; pc st in next sp, (ch 2, dc in next sp) twice; pc st in next dc, dc in top of next pc st, dc in next 3 dc, in next sp make dc, ch 3 and dc; dc in next 3 dc, dc in top of next pc st, pc st in next dc. Repeat from * around, ending with dc in last sp, pc st in last dc. Join and fasten off.

Make necessary number of motifs and sew together on wrong side with neat over-and-over stitches, joining them as in diagram for joining hexagon motifs. For single size spread make 17 motifs from A to B and 20 motifs from A to C; for double size spread make 21 motifs from A to B and 20 motifs from A to C.

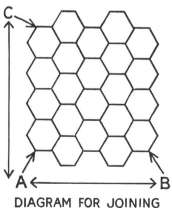

DIAGRAM FOR JOINING HEXAGON MOTIFS

Doilies

Sea Shells

The shell motif echoes the beauty of the sea
. . . against a background of blue linen.

DIRECTIONS ON PAGE 61.

Shining Star

ROYAL SOCIETY SIX CORD CORDICHET, Large Ball,
Size 20, 8 balls of White or Ecru.

Steel Crochet Hook No. 9.

Doily measures 30 inches in diameter.

Starting at center, ch 10. Join with sl st to form ring. **1st rnd:** Ch 7, (tr in ring, ch 3) 7 times. Join to 4th ch of ch-7. **2nd rnd:** Ch 4, * 4 tr in next sp, tr in next tr. Repeat from * around. Join. **3rd rnd:** Sc in same place as sl st, * ch 5, sc in next tr. Repeat from * around. Join. **4th, 5th and 6th rnds:** Sl st to center of next loop, sc in same loop, * ch 7, sc in next loop. Repeat from * around. Join. **7th rnd:** Sl st to center of next loop, ch 4, 2 tr in same loop, * (ch 7, sc in next loop) 4 times; ch 7, 3 tr in next loop. Repeat from * around. Join. **8th rnd:** Sl st in next tr, ch 4, in same tr make 2 tr, ch 3 and 3 tr (shell made); * ch 2, 3 tr in next loop, (ch 7, sc in next loop) 3 times; ch 7, 3 tr in next loop, ch 2, skip 1 tr, in next tr

make 3 tr, ch 3 and 3 tr (another shell made). Repeat from * around. Join. **9th rnd:** Sl st in next 2 tr, sl st in next sp, ch 4, in same sp make 2 tr, ch 3 and 3 tr (shell made over shell); * ch 2, skip next sp, tr in next 3 tr, 3 tr in next loop, (ch 7, sc in next loop) twice; ch 7, 3 tr in next loop, tr in next 3 tr, ch 2, shell in sp of next shell. Repeat from * around. Join. **10th rnd:** * Shell over shell, ch 2, skip next sp, tr in next 6 tr, 3 tr in next loop, ch 7, sc in next loop, ch 7, 3 tr in next loop, tr in next 6 tr, ch 2. Repeat from * around. Join. **11th rnd:** * Shell over shell, ch 2, skip next sp, tr in next 9 tr, 3 tr in next loop, ch 2, 3 tr in next loop, tr in the next 9 tr, ch 2. Repeat from * around. Join.

12th rnd: * Shell over shell, ch 2, skip

next sp, tr in next 12 tr, 3 tr in next sp, tr in next 12 tr, ch 2. Repeat from * around. Join. **13th rnd:** * Shell over shell, ch 2, skip next sp, tr in next 13 tr, in next tr make tr, ch 5 and tr; tr in next 13 tr, ch 2. Repeat from * around. Join. **14th rnd:** * Shell over shell, ch 2, skip next sp, tr in next 12 tr, ch 2, 9 tr in next sp, ch 2, tr in next 12 tr, ch 2. Repeat from * around. Join. **15th rnd:** * Shell over shell, ch 2, skip next sp, tr in next 10 tr, ch 5, skip next 2 tr, (sc in next tr, ch 5) 9 times; skip 2 tr, tr in next 10 tr, ch 2. Repeat from * around. Join. **16th rnd:** * Shell over shell, ch 2, skip next sp, tr in next 8 tr, ch 7, skip next sp, (sc in next loop, ch 7) 8 times; skip 2 tr, tr in next 8 tr, ch 2. Repeat from * around. Join. **17th rnd:** * Shell

over shell, ch 2, skip next sp, tr in next 8 tr, 3 tr in next loop, (ch 7, sc in next loop) 7 times; ch 7, 3 tr in next loop, tr in next 8 tr, ch 2. Repeat from * around. Join. **18th rnd:** * Shell over shell, ch 2, skip next sp, tr in next 11 tr, 3 tr in next loop, (ch 7, sc in next loop) 6 times; ch 7, 3 tr in next loop, tr in next 11 tr, ch 2. Repeat from * around. Join. **19th rnd:** * Shell over shell, ch 2, skip next sp, tr in next 14 tr, 3 tr in next loop, (ch 7, sc in next loop) 5 times; ch 7, 3 tr in next loop, tr in next 14 tr, ch 2. Repeat from * around. Join. **20th rnd:** * Shell over shell, ch 2, skip next sp, tr in next 17 tr, 3 tr in next loop, (ch 7, sc in next loop) 4 times; ch 7, 3 tr in next loop, tr in next 17 tr, ch 2. Repeat from * around. Join. **21st rnd:** * Shell over shell, ch 2, skip next sp, tr in next 20 tr, 3 tr in next loop, (ch 7, sc in next loop) 3 times; ch 7, 3 tr in next loop, tr in next 20 tr, ch 2. Repeat from * around. Join. **22nd rnd:** * Shell over shell, ch 2, skip next sp, tr in next 23 tr, 3 tr in next loop, (ch 7, sc in next loop) twice; ch 7, 3 tr in next loop, tr in next 23 tr, ch 2. Repeat from * around. Join. **23rd rnd:** * Shell over shell, ch 2, skip next sp, tr in next 26 tr, 3 tr in next loop, ch 7, sc in next loop, ch 7, 3 tr in next loop, tr in next 26 tr, ch 2. Repeat from * around. Join. **24th rnd:** * Shell over shell, ch 2, skip next sp, tr in next 29 tr, 3 tr in each of next 2 sps, tr in next 29 tr, ch 2. Repeat from * around. Join.

25th rnd: * Shell over shell, ch 2, skip next sp, tr in next 3 tr, (ch 2, skip 2 tr, tr in next tr) 9 times; tr in next 2 tr, ch 5, tr in next 3 tr, (ch 2, skip next 2 tr, tr in next tr) 9 times; tr in next 2 tr, ch 2. Repeat from * around. Join. **26th**

rnd: * Shell over shell, ch 2, skip next sp, 2 tr in next tr, tr in next 2 tr, (ch 2, tr in next tr) 7 times; ch 2, skip next sp, 3 tr in next sp, 9 tr in next sp, ch 2, 3 tr in next sp, ch 2, skip next tr, (tr in next tr, ch 2) 7 times; tr in next 2 tr, 2 tr in next tr, ch 2. Repeat from * around. Join. **27th rnd:** * Shell over shell, ch 2, skip next sp, 2 tr in next tr, tr in next 3 tr, (ch 2, tr in next tr) 6 times; ch 2, skip next sp, 3 tr in next sp, ch 5, skip next sp, (sc in next tr, ch 5) 9 times; skip next sp, 3 tr in next sp, ch 2, skip next tr, (tr in next tr, ch 2) 6 times; tr in next 3 tr, 2 tr in next tr, ch 2. Repeat from * around. Join. **28th rnd:** * Shell over shell, ch 2, skip next sp, 2 tr in next tr, tr in next 4 tr, (ch 2, tr in next tr) 5 times; ch 2, skip next sp, 3 tr in next sp, ch 7, skip next sp, (sc in next loop, ch 7) 8 times; skip next sp, 3 tr in next sp, ch 2, skip next tr, (tr in next tr, ch 2) 5 times; tr in next 4 tr, 2 tr in next tr, ch 2. Repeat from * around. Join. **29th rnd:** * Shell over shell, ch 2, skip next sp, 2 tr in next tr, tr in next 5 tr, (ch 2, tr in next tr) 6 times; ch 2, 3 tr in next sp, (ch 7, sc in next loop) 7 times; ch 7, 3 tr in next sp, ch 2, skip 2 tr, (tr in next tr, ch 2) 6 times; tr in next 5 tr, 2 tr in next tr, ch 2. Repeat from * around. Join. **30th rnd:** Sl st to sp of shell, ch 4, in same sp make 2 tr, (ch 3, 3 tr) twice; * ch 2, skip next sp, 2 tr in next tr, tr in next 6 tr, (ch 2, tr in next tr) 7 times; ch 2, 3 tr in next loop, (ch 7, sc in next loop) 6 times; ch 7, 3 tr in next loop, ch 2, skip 2 tr, (tr in next tr, ch 2) 8 times; tr in next 6 tr, 2 tr in next tr, ch 2, in sp of next shell make (3 tr, ch 3) twice and 3 tr. Repeat from * around. Join.

Now work in rows as follows: **1st row:** Sl st in next 2 tr, across next sp and in

next 3 tr, sl st in next sp, ch 4, in same sp make 2 tr, ch 3 and 3 tr; ch 1, skip next sp and 2 tr, tr in next 6 tr, (2 tr in next sp, tr in next tr) 8 times; tr in next 2 tr, 3 tr in next loop, (ch 7, sc in next loop) 5 times; ch 7, 3 tr in next loop, tr in next 3 tr, (2 tr in next sp, tr in next tr) 8 times; tr in next 5 tr, ch 1, skip next sp, shell in next sp. Turn. **2nd row:** Sl st in next 3 tr, sl st in sp, shell over shell, ch 1, skip 3 tr, tr in each tr across, 3 tr in next loop, (ch 7, sc in next loop) 4 times; ch 7, 3 tr in next loop, tr in each tr across to within last 3 tr, ch 1, shell over shell. Turn. **3rd and 4th rows:** Repeat last row having 1 loop less on pineapple on each row. **5th row:** Shell over shell, ch 1, skip 3 tr, tr in each tr across, 3 tr in next loop, ch 7, sc in next loop, ch 7, 3 tr in next loop, tr in each tr across to within last 3 tr, ch 1, shell over shell. Turn. **6th row:** Shell over shell, ch 1, skip 3 tr, tr in each tr across,. 3 tr in next loop, ch 1, 3 tr in next loop, tr in each tr across to within last 3 tr, ch 1, shell over shell. Turn. **7th row:** Shell over shell, ch 1, skip 3 tr, tr in each tr across, 3 tr in ch-1 sp, tr in each tr across to within last 3 tr, ch 1, shell over shell. Turn. **8th to 22nd rows incl:** Shell over shell, ch 1, skip 3 tr, tr in each tr across to center tr of 3-tr group, 3 tr in center tr, tr in each remaining tr across to within last 3 tr, ch 1, shell over shell. Turn. **23rd row:** Shell over shell, skip 3 tr, 3 tr in next tr, shell over shell. Turn. **24th row:** Shell over next 2 shells. Break off. Attach thread to next sp on 30th rnd and work remaining points to correspond. Starch lightly and press.

Sea Shells

ILLUSTRATED ON PAGE 59.

MATERIALS:

J. & P. Coats Best Six Cord Mercerized Crochet, Art. A.104, Size 50: 1 ball of White . . . Milwards Steel Crochet Hook No. 12 . . . A piece of blue linen, 9½ inches in diameter.

Centerpiece measures 18 inches in diameter.

Make a narrow hem all around linen. **1st rnd:** Attach thread to edge of linen and sc closely around, having 390 sc on rnd (about 14 sc to 1 inch). Join with sl st to first sc. **2nd rnd:** Sc in same place as sl st, sc in next 3 sc, * ch 4, skip 2 sc, sc in next 4 sc. Repeat from * around. Join (65 ch-4 sps on rnd). **3rd rnd:** Ch 6, * sc in

next 2 sc, ch 3, 4 dc in next loop, ch 3, skip next sc. Repeat from * around, ending with 3 dc in last loop, sl st in 3rd ch of ch-6. **4th rnd:** * Ch 4, sc in next 4 dc. Repeat from * around. Join. **5th rnd:** Sl st in next sp, ch 3, 3 dc in same sp, * ch 3, skip next sc, sc in next 2 sc, ch 3, 4 dc in next sp. Repeat from * around. Join to top of starting ch-3. **6th rnd:** Sc in same place as sl st, sc in next 3 dc, * ch 4, sc in next 4 dc. Repeat from * around. Join. **7th rnd:** Repeat 3rd rnd. **8th rnd:** Repeat 4th rnd. **9th rnd:** Ch 3, make 3 dc in each sp and dc in each sc around. Join to top of ch-3 (456 dc on rnd, counting starting ch-3 as 1 dc). **10th rnd:** * Sc in next 13 dc, ch 8, skip next 6 dc, dc in next 13 dc, ch 8, skip next 6 dc. Repeat from * around. Join. **11th rnd:** Sl st in next sc, sc in same sc and in next 11 sc (1 sc decreased

on this sc-section), * ch 8, (dc in next dc, ch 1) 12 times; dc in next dc, ch 8, skip next sc, sc in next 12 sc. Repeat from * around. Join. **12th rnd:** Sl st in next sc, sc in same place as sl st, * sc in each remaining sc on this section, ch 8, (dc in next dc, ch 2) 12 times; dc in next dc, ch 8, skip 1 sc. Repeat from * around. Join. **13th to 22nd rnds incl:** Work as for 12th rnd, having 1 sc less on each sc-section on every rnd and having 1 more ch between dc's of each dc-section on every other rnd (ch 7 on 22nd rnd). **23rd rnd:** Sl st to center of next sp, sc in same sp, * (ch 7, sl st in 4th ch from hook—picot made—ch 3, sc in next sp) 13 times; sc in next sp, ch 1, sc in first sp of next scallop. Repeat from * around. Join and break off.

Starch lightly and press.

Floral Splendor

MATERIALS:

Clark's O.N.T. Best Six Cord Mercerized Crochet, Art. B.4, Size 30: 8 balls of White . . . Milwards Steel Crochet Hook No. 10 . . . A piece of linen, 6 inches in diameter.

Centerpiece measures 16 inches in diameter.

FIRST MOTIF . . . Starting at center, ch 8. Join with sl st to form ring. **1st rnd:** Ch 9, (tr in ring, ch 5) 7 times. Join with sl st to 4th ch of ch-9. **2nd rnd:** 8 sc in each ch-5 sp around. Join. **3rd rnd:** Ch 3, dc in next sc and in each sc around. Join. **4th rnd:** Ch 4, holding back on hook the last loop of each tr make tr in next 2 dc, thread over and draw through all loops on hook (a 2-tr cluster made); * ch 6, skip next dc, 3-tr cluster over next 3 dc. Repeat from * around, ending with ch 6, sl st in top of ch-4 (16 clusters on rnd). **5th rnd:** 8 sc in each sp around. Join. **6th rnd:** Sl st in next sc, ch 3, dc in next 11 sc, * ch 5,

skip 4 sc, dc in next 12 sc. Repeat from * around, ending with ch 5. Join to top of ch-3. **7th rnd:** Ch 3, dc in next 11 dc, * ch 5, sc in next sp, ch 5, dc in next 12 dc. Repeat from * around. Join. **8th rnd:** Ch 3, * dc in each dc of this dc section, (ch 5, sc in next loop) twice; ch 5. Repeat from * around. Join. **9th rnd:** Sl st in next 2 dc, ch 3, dc in next 7 dc, * (ch 5, sc in next loop) 3 times; ch 5, skip next 2 dc, dc in next 8 dc. Repeat from * around. Join. **10th rnd:** Sl st in next 2 dc, ch 3, dc in next 3 dc, * (ch 5, sc in next loop) 4 times; ch 5, skip next 2 dc, dc in next 4 dc. Repeat from * around (8 points on rnd). Join and break off.

SECOND MOTIF . . . Work as for First Motif until 9 rnds have been completed. **10th rnd:** Work as for 10th rnd of First Motif until 7 points have been completed, ch 2, sl st in last ch-5 loop on any ch-5 loop section on First Motif, (ch 2, sc in next loop on Second Motif, ch 2, sl st in next loop on First

Motif) 4 times; ch 2, skip next 2 dc, dc in next 4 dc and complete rnd as for First Motif (no more joinings).

Make 5 more Motifs, joining adjacent sides as Second Motif was joined to First Motif and leaving 20 loops free on outer edge and 10 loops free on inner edge between joinings. Join first and last motifs.

OUTER EDGE . . . 1st rnd: Attach thread to ch-2 sp preceding joining on any motif, sc in same place, * sc in corresponding ch-2 sp following joining on next motif, (ch 5, sc in next loop) 20 times; ch 5, sc in ch-2 sp preceding joining. Repeat from * around. Join. **2nd rnd:** Make 7 sc in each ch-5 loop around. Join. **3rd rnd:** Sl st in next 2 sc, ch 4, 2-tr cluster over next 2 sc, * ch 6, skip last 2 sc of this 7-sc group and next 2 sc of next 7-sc group, make a 3-tr cluster over next 3 sc. Repeat from * across motif, ending with a 3-tr cluster over last 7-sc group on motif, make a 3-tr

Continued on page 63

Trio Tricks

MATERIALS—DAISY Mercerized Crochet Cotton size 30: —1 skein White, Cream or Ecru. Crochet hook size 12. Size—9½".

Ch 10, sl st in 1st st. Ch 1, 12 sc in ring. In back lps, sl st in 1st sc, ch 17, sc in 5th st from hook for a p, ch 1, a long tr (thread over 5 times and work off in twos) in same sc, (ch 5, p, ch 1, a long tr in next sc, ch 5, p, ch 1, a long tr in same sc) repeated around, joining final p-lp to 11th st of 1st lp (24 ps). **ROW 3**—Ch 7, dc in next long tr, (ch 4, dc in next long tr) repeated around. Join to 3d st of 1st 7-ch. **ROW 4**—Ch 1, (5 sc in next sp, 1 sc in dc) repeated around. Sl st in 1st 1-ch. **ROW 5**—Ch 17, p, ch 1, a long tr in next 3d sc, (ch 5, p, ch 1, a long tr in next 3d sc) repeated around and join to 11th st of 1st lp. Repeat Row 3. **ROW 7**—Ch 1, (4 sc in next sp, 1 sc in dc) repeated around. Sl st in 1st 1-ch. **ROW 8**—** (Ch 4, sc in next 2d sc) 12 times, ch 2, dc in next 2 dc, sc. * Turn, (ch 4, sc in next lp) repeated across to 2d from end, ch 2, dc in end lp. Repeat from * 11 times (1 lp in final row). Cut 2" long. Join to next 4th sc on center and repeat from ** around. **ROW**

9—* 7 sc in tip sp of one point, (3 sc in next sp) 12 times, working over end left from point, sl st between points, (3 sc in next sp) 4 times, ch 8, turn, sl st in 12th sc up side of last point, ch 1, turn, (5 sc, ch 5, sl st in last sc for a p, and 5 sc) in lp, (3 sc in next sp) 3 times, ch 22, turn, sl st in next 9th sc up side of last point, ch 1, turn, 29 sc in lp, (3 sc in next sp) 5 times. Repeat from * around. **ROW 10**— Sl st in 1st 7 sc, * ch 5, p, ch 1, a long tr (thread over 6 times and work off in twos) in 1st sc on lp between points, (ch 5, p, ch 1, a long tr in next 2d sc) 14 times, ch 5 p, ch 1, sl st in 7th sc in tip of next point. Repeat from * around. **ROW 11**—Sl st to tip of point, * (ch 4, dc in next long tr) 15 times, ch 4, sc in tip of point. Repeat from * around. **ROW 12**—Ch 1, (4 sc in next sp, 1 sc in next st) repeated around, sl st in 1st 1-ch. **ROW 13**—Ch 13, a 2-tr-Cluster in 6th st from hook, ch 1, sc in next 10th sc (directly above a dc), * ch 6, a 2-tr-Cluster in 6th st from hook, tr in next 5th sc, ch 5, sl st in tr for a p, ch 6, a Cluster, ch 1, sc in next 5th sc. Repeat from * 5 times. Ch 6, a Cluster, dtr in sc between shells, a p, ch 6, a Cluster, ch 1, sc in next 10th sc. Repeat from * around. Join final Cluster to 7th st of 1st lp, a p and fasten off. Stretch and pin right-side-down in a true circle. Steam and press dry thru a cloth.

Floral Splendor

Continued from page 62

cluster over first 7-sc group on next motif (thus omitting the ch-6 loop) and complete rnd to correspond. Join to tip of first cluster. **4th rnd:** In each ch-6 loop around make 4 sc, ch 5, sl st in 5th ch from hook (picot made) and 4 sc. Join and break off.

INNER EDGE . . . 1st rnd: Attach thread to any joining between motifs, * (ch 5, sc in next loop) 10 times; ch 5, sc in next joining. Repeat from * around. Join. **2nd rnd:** 5 sc in each loop around. Join with sl st to first sc. **3rd rnd:** Sl st in next 12 sc, ch 9, * (tr in center sc of next loop, ch 5) twice; dc in center sc of next loop, ch 5, (tr in center sc of next loop, ch 5) twice; holding back on hook the last loop of each d tr, make a d tr in

center sc of next loop, skip 2 loops on next motif, d tr in center sc of next loop, thread over and draw through all loops on hook (joint d tr made), ch 5. Repeat from * around. Join last d tr to 5th ch of ch-9. Break off.

Pin in place on linen and trace outline of center. Cut linen leaving ¼ inch for hem. Roll hem and sew neatly in place. Sew inner edge to linen. Starch lightly and press.

Cluster Stitch Doily

Materials Required: AMERICAN THREAD COMPANY
The Famous "PURITAN" MERCERIZED CROCHET COTTON, Article 40
3 balls White
Steel crochet hook No. 7
Approximate size: 22 inches in diameter or
"GEM" MERCERIZED CROCHET COTTON, Article 35, size 30
2 balls White
Steel crochet hook No. 12
Approximate size: 16 inches in diameter

General Notations: A cluster st at beginning of each round is made as follows: ch 3 (to count as 1 d c), 2 more d c in same space, keeping last loop of each d c on hook, thread over and work off all loops at one time (this completes a cluster st at beginning of the round).

The regular cluster sts through 1st 12 rounds of doily are made as follows: 3 d c in same space keeping last loop of each d c on hook, thread over and work off all loops at one time.

Ch 9, join to form a ring, work 8 cluster sts with ch 4 between each cluster st in ring, ch 4, join in top of 1st cluster st.

2nd Round: Sl st into loop, work 2 cluster sts with ch 3 between in same space, ° ch 3, 2 cluster sts with ch 3 between in next loop, repeat from ° all around, ch 3, join.

3rd Round: Cluster st in 1st cluster st, ° ch 3, cluster st in next loop, ch 3, cluster st in top of next cluster st, ch 3, skip next ch 3 loop, cluster st in top of next cluster st, repeat from ° all around ending with ch 3, cluster st in next loop, ch 3, cluster st in top of next cluster st, ch 3, join.

4th Round: Cluster st in 1st cluster st, ° ch 3, 2 cluster sts with ch 3 between in next cluster st, ch 3, cluster st in next cluster st, ch 3, cluster st in next cluster st, repeat from ° all around ending to correspond, ch 3, join.

5th Round: Cluster st in 1st cluster st, ch 3, cluster st in next cluster st, ° ch 3, cluster st in next loop, ch 3, 1 cluster st in each of the next 4 cluster sts with ch 3 between each cluster st, repeat from ° all around ending to correspond, ch 3, join.

6th Round: ° 1 cluster st in each of the next 5 cluster sts with ch 3 between each cluster st, ch 5, repeat from ° all around, join.

7th Round: ° 1 cluster st in each of the next 5 cluster sts with ch 3 between each cluster st, ch 9, repeat from ° all around, join.

8th Round: Cluster st in 1st cluster st, ° ch 3, cluster st in next cluster st, ch 1, cluster st in next cluster st, ch 1, cluster st in next cluster st, ch 3, cluster st in next cluster st, ch 6, d c in center st of next loop, ch 6, cluster st in next cluster st, repeat from ° all around to correspond, join.

9th Round: Cluster st in 1st cluster st, ° ch 3, cluster st in next cluster st, ch 1, skip 1 cluster st, cluster st in next cluster st, ch 3, cluster st in next cluster st, ch 6, d c in next d c, ch 7, d c in same space, ch 6, cluster st in next cluster st, repeat from ° all around ending to correspond, join.

10th Round: Cluster st in 1st cluster st, ° ch 1, skip 1 loop, cluster st in next ch 1 space, ch 1, skip 1 loop, cluster st in next cluster st, ch 7, d c in next d c, ch 7, d c in center st of next loop, ch 7, d c in next d c, ch 7, cluster st in next cluster st, repeat from ° all around to correspond, join.

11th Round: Cluster st in 1st cluster, ° ch 1, skip 1 cluster st, cluster st in next cluster st, ch 7, d c in next d c, ch 7, d c in next d c, ch 5, d c in same space, ch 7, d c in next d c, ch 7, cluster st in next cluster st, repeat from ° all around ending to correspond, join.

12th Round: Sl st into ch 1 space, cluster st in same space, ° ch 12, s c in next d c, ch 12, skip 1 loop, s c in next ch 5 loop, ch 12, skip 1 loop, s c in next d c, ch 12, cluster st in next ch 1 space, repeat from ° all around ending to correspond, join.

13th Round: Sl st to center of next loop, ch 4 (counts as part of 1st tr c cluster st), 2 tr c in same space keeping last loop of each tr c on hook, thread over and work off all loops at one time, ° ch 11, 2 tr c in next loop, ch 11, 3 tr c cluster st in next loop (tr c cluster st: 3 tr c in same space keeping last loop of each tr c on hook, thread over and work off all loops at one time), repeat from ° all around ending with ch 11, 2 tr c in next loop, ch 11, join.

14th Round: Ch 4 (always counts as part of 1st cluster st), tr c cluster st in same space, ° ch 5, 5 tr c in next tr c, ch 2, tr c in same space, tr c in next tr c, ch 2, 5 tr c in same space, ch 5, 3 tr c cluster st in next cluster st, repeat from ° all around ending to correspond, ch 5, join.

15th Round: Ch 4, tr c cluster st in same space, ° ch 1, tr c cluster st in same space, ch 4, 1 tr c in each of the next 5 tr c keeping last loop of each tr c on hook, thread over and work off all loops at one time, ch 5, 3 tr c in next tr c, 2 tr c in next tr c, ch 5, 1 tr c in each of the next 5 tr c keeping last loop of each tr c on hook, thread over and work off all loops at one time, ch 4, tr c cluster st in next cluster st, repeat from ° all around ending to correspond, ch 4, join in 1st cluster st.

16th Round: Ch 4, tr c cluster st in same space, ° ch 4, tr c in next ch 1 space, ch 4, tr c cluster st in next tr c cluster st, ch 7, skip 2 loops, 1 s c in each of the next 5 tr c, ch 7, skip 2 loops, tr c cluster st in next tr c cluster st, repeat from ° all around ending to correspond, ch 7, join.

17th Round: Ch 4, tr c cluster st in same space, ° ch 6, tr c in next tr c, ch 6, tr c cluster st in next tr c cluster st, ch 7, 1 tr c in each of the next 5 s c keeping last loop of each tr c on hook, thread over and work off all loops at one time (5 tr c cluster), ch 7, skip 1 loop, tr c cluster st in next tr c cluster st, repeat from ° all around ending to correspond, ch 7, join.

18th Round: Ch 4, tr c cluster st in same space, ° ch 8, 1 tr c, ch 3, 1 tr c in next tr c, ch 8, tr c cluster st in next tr c cluster st, ch 6, s c in next 5 tr c cluster, ch 6, tr c cluster st in next tr c cluster st, repeat from ° all around ending to correspond, ch 6, join.

All cluster sts are tr c cluster sts for remainder of doily and will be referred to as cluster sts only.

19th Round: Ch 4, cluster st in same space, ° ch 8, 5 tr c in next tr c, ch 2, 2 tr c in next ch 3 loop, ch 2, 5 tr c in next tr c, ch 8, cluster st in next cluster st, ch 6, s c in next s c, ch 6, cluster st in next cluster st, repeat from ° all around ending to correspond, join.

20th Round: Ch 4, cluster st in same space, ch 8, sl st in top of cluster st for picot, ° ch 8, 5 tr c cluster over next 5 tr c, ch 5, 5 tr c in next tr c, ch 2, tr c in same space, tr c in next tr c, ch 2, 5 tr c in same space, ch 5, 5 tr c cluster over next 5 tr c, ch 8, cluster st in next cluster st, ch 8, sl st in top of cluster st for picot, cluster st in next cluster st (this closes the point), repeat from ° all around ending with ch 8, 5 tr c cluster over next 5 tr c, ch 5, 5 tr c in next tr c, ch 2, tr c in same space, tr c in next tr c, ch 2, 5 tr c in same space, ch 5, 5 tr c cluster over next 5 tr c, ch 8, cluster st in next cluster st, join in next cluster st.

21st Round: Sl st into picot, ch 4, cluster st in same space, ch 7, cluster st in same space, ° ch 8, skip 2 loops, 5 tr c cluster over next 5 tr c, ch 5, 5 tr c in next tr c, ch 2, tr c in same space, tr c in next tr c, ch 2, 5 tr c in same space, ch 5, 5

tr c cluster over next 5 tr c, ch 8, skip 2 loops, 2 cluster sts with ch 7 between in next picot, repeat from * all around ending to correspond, join.

22nd Round: Ch 4, cluster st in same space, * ch 5, cluster st in next loop, ch 5, cluster st in next cluster st, ch 7, skip 2 loops, 5 tr c cluster over next 5 tr c, ch 7, 3 tr c in next tr c, 2 tr c in next tr c, ch 7, 5 tr c cluster over next 5 tr c, ch 7, skip 2 loops, cluster st in next cluster st, repeat from * all around ending to correspond, join.

23rd Round: Ch 4, cluster st in same space, ch 3, cluster st in same space, * ch 4, 2 cluster sts with ch 3 between in next cluster st, ch 4, 2 cluster sts with ch 3 between in next cluster st, ch 10, skip 2 loops, 1 s c in each of the next 5 tr c, ch 10, skip 2 loops, 2 cluster sts with ch 3 between in next cluster st, repeat from * all around ending to correspond, join.

24th Round: Ch 4, cluster st in same space, * ch 3, cluster st in next loop, ch 3, cluster st in next cluster st, ch 4, cluster st in next cluster st, repeat from * once, ch 3, cluster st in next loop, ch 3, cluster st in next cluster st, ch 9, 5 tr c cluster over next 5 s c, ch 9, skip 1 loop, cluster st in next cluster st, repeat from first * all around ending to correspond, join.

25th Round: Ch 4, cluster st in same space, ** ch 3, cluster st in next cluster st, ch 3, cluster st in next cluster st, * ch 4, 1 cluster st in each of the next 3 cluster sts with ch 3 between each cluster st, repeat from * once, ch 8, s c in next 5 tr c cluster, ch 8, cluster st in next cluster st, repeat from ** all around ending to correspond, join.

26th Round: Ch 4, cluster st in same space, ** ch 2, cluster st in next cluster st, ch 2, cluster st in next cluster st, * ch 4, 1 tr c, ch 3, 1 tr c in next loop, ch 4, cluster st in next cluster st, ch 2, cluster st in next cluster st, ch 2, cluster st in next cluster st, repeat from * once, ch 8, s c in next s c, ch 8, cluster st in next cluster st, repeat from ** all around ending to correspond, join.

27th Round: Ch 4, cluster st in same space, * skip 1 cluster st, cluster st in next cluster st, ch 4, tr c in next tr c, ch 4, tr c in next loop, ch 4, tr c in next tr c, ch 4, cluster st in next cluster st, repeat from * once, skip 1 cluster st, cluster st in next cluster st, ch 4, tr c in 1st cluster st of next cluster st group, ch 4, cluster st in same space, repeat from 1st * all around ending to correspond, join in 1st cluster st.

28th Round: Sl st between 1st 2 cluster sts, ch 11, sl st in 6th st from hook for picot, ch 7, sl st in same space, ch 6, sl st in same space, tr c between same 2 cluster sts, * ch 6, s c in next tr c, ch 6, tr c in next tr c, ch 6, sl st in top of tr c for picot, ch 7, sl st in same space, ch 6, sl st in same space (3 picot group), tr c in same space with tr c, ch 6, s c in next tr c, ch 6, tr c between next 2 cluster sts, work a 3 picot group, tr c in same space with last tr c, ch 6, s c in next tr c, ch 6, tr c in next tr c, work a 3 picot group, tr c in same space with last tr c, ch 6, s c in next tr c, ch 6, tr c between next 2 cluster sts, work a 3 picot group, tr c in same space with last tr c, ch 6, s c between next 2 tr c, ch 6, tr c between next 2 cluster sts, work a 3 picot group, tr c in same space with last tr c, repeat from * all around ending to correspond, join, cut thread.

Rock Pool

A scalloped shell pattern that is so simple to make,

yet has an air of fragile grace . . . .

**J. & P. COATS BIG BALL BEST SIX CORD MERCERIZED
CROCHET, Art. A.104,** Size 30: 3 balls of Ecru; or
CLARK'S BIG BALL MERCERIZED CROCHET, Art. B.34,
Size 30: 3 balls of No. 61 Ecru.

Milwards Steel Crochet Hook No. 10.

Doily measures 15 inches in diameter, including ruffle.

Starting at center, ch 10. Join with sl st to form
ring. **1st rnd:** 24 sc in ring. Join. **2nd rnd:** Ch 5, * tr in
next sc, ch 1. Repeat from * around. Join with sl st to
4th ch of ch-5. **3rd rnd:** Sc in same place as sl st,
* sc in next sp, sc in next tr. Repeat from * around.
Join (48 sc). **4th and 5th rnds:** Repeat 2nd and 3rd
rnds (96 sc on 5th rnd). **6th rnd:** Ch 4, tr in each sc
around. Join. **7th rnd:** Sc in same place as sl st, sc in
each tr around. Join. **8th rnd:** Sc in same place as sl st,
* (ch 5, skip 2 sc, sc in next sc) twice; ch 5, skip 1 sc,
sc in next sc. Repeat from * around, ending with
ch 2, dc in first sc (36 loops). **9th rnd:** In loop just
formed make sc, ch 3 and sc (picot made); * ch 5, in
next loop make sc, ch 3 and sc (another picot). Repeat
from * around, ending with ch 2, dc in first sc. **10th
to 17th rnds incl:** Make a picot in loop just formed,
* ch 5, make a picot in next ch-5 loop. Repeat from *
around. Join as before. At end of 17th rnd, join last
ch-5 with sl st to first sc. **18th rnd:** Sl st in picot, ch 3,
2 dc in same place (shell made); * picot in next ch-5
loop, 3-dc shell in next picot. Repeat from * around.
Join.

19th rnd: Sl st in next dc, picot in same place, * shell
in next picot, picot in center dc of next shell. Repeat
from * around. Join. **20th rnd:** Sl st in next picot,
ch 3, 4 dc in same place, * picot in center dc of next
shell, 5-dc shell in next picot. Repeat from * around.
Join. **21st rnd:** Work as for 19th rnd, making 5 dc in
each shell instead of 3 dc. **22nd rnd:** Repeat 20th rnd.
23rd rnd: Work as for 19th rnd, making 7 dc in each
shell. **24th rnd:** Sl st in next picot, ch 3, 6 dc in same
place, (picot in center dc of next shell, 7-dc shell in
next picot) twice; * picot in next shell, draw loop on

Continued on page 78

Sea Scallop

Materials Required:

AMERICAN THREAD COMPANY

The Famous "PURITAN" MERCERIZED STAR
  SPANGLED CROCHET COTTON, Article 40
4 balls Silver Spangle or

The Famous "PURITAN" MERCERIZED
  CROCHET COTTON, Article 40
2 balls White or color of your choice

Steel Crochet hook No. 7

App. size: 19½ inches in diameter for "PURITAN"
  STAR SPANGLED; 19½ inches in diameter for
  "PURITAN"

Chain (ch) 5, slip stitch (sl st) in 1st stitch (st) of ch for picot, ch 4, 3 double crochet (dc) in 1st st of ch, repeat from beginning 3 times, join. 2nd ROUND: Ch 7, double treble crochet (d trc: 3 times over hook) in same space, * ch 2, d trc in same space, repeat from * 7 times, * 9 d trc with ch 2 between each d trc in next picot, repeat from * twice, join. 3rd ROUND: 2 single crochet (sc) in same loop, * ch 1, 2 sc in next loop, repeat from * 6 times, ch 1, * 2 sc in next loop, ch 1, repeat from * 7 times, complete round to correspond, join in 1st sc. 4th ROUND: Sl st to 1st ch 1, * ch 5, sc in next ch 1, repeat from * 5 times, ch 5, skip next ch 1, sc in next ch 1, complete round to correspond ending with ch 2, dc in 1st sc (this brings thread in position for next round). 5th to 9th ROUND: Ch 3, sc in same space, * ch 5, sc in next loop, ch 3,

sc in same loop, repeat from * all around ending with dc in dc. 10th ROUND: Ch 3, dc in same space, * ch 4, 2 dc in next ch 5 loop, repeat from * all around, join in 3rd st of ch. 11th ROUND: Ch 3, dc in next dc, * 4 dc in next loop, 1 dc in each of the next 2 dc, repeat from * all around ending with 4 dc in last loop, join in 3rd st of ch. 12th ROUND: Ch 4, treble crochet (trc) in same space, 2 trc in next dc, * ch 5, skip 4 dc, sc in next dc, ch 5, sc in next dc, ch 5, skip 5 trc, 2 trc in each of the next 2 dc, repeat from beginning all around ending to correspond, join in 4th st of ch. 13th ROUND: Ch 4, trc in same space, 1 trc in each of the next 2 trc, 2 trc in next trc, * ch 5, skip next loop, sc in next loop, ch 5, sc in same loop, ch 5, 2 trc in next trc, 1 trc in each of the next 2 trc, 2 trc in last trc, repeat from * all around ending to correspond, join. 14th and 15th ROUNDS: Same as last round working 2 trc in 1st and last trc, and 1 trc in each trc between in each of the 14 trc groups. 16th ROUND: Ch 4, 3 trc in same space, 1 trc in each of the next 8 trc, 4 trc in last trc, * ch 1, skip 1 loop, sc in next loop, ch 1, 4 trc in next trc, 1 trc in each of the next 8 trc, 4 trc in last trc, repeat from * all around ending to correspond, join. 17th ROUND: Ch 5, skip 1 trc, sc in next trc, repeat from beginning twice, ch 5, skip 2 trc, sc in next trc, * ch 5, skip 1 trc, sc in next trc, repeat from * twice, sc in next trc, repeat from beginning

Continued on page 79

2203

2204

2205

Three's Company

DOILY No. 2203

Materials Required—AMERICAN THREAD COMPANY "STAR" or "GEM" MERCERIZED CROCHET COTTON, Size 20 or 30

1—300 Yd. Ball White or Colors.
Steel Crochet Hook No. 11 or 12.
Each Motif measures about 4 inches. 7 motifs are required for doily illustrated. Doily measures about 10 inches through the center.

Motif. Ch 6, join to form a ring, ch 6, d c into ring, * ch 3, d c into ring, repeat from * 3 times, ch 3, sl st into 3rd st of 6 ch loop to join.

2nd Row. Ch 3, 2 d c in same space, * ch 5, sl st into 4th st from hook for picot, ch 1, 3 d c in next d c, repeat from * 4 times, picot loop and sl st into ch 3 to join.

3rd Row. Ch 3, 1 d c in each of the next 2 d c, * ch 5, sl st in 4th st from hook for picot, ch 5, sl st in 4th st from hook for picot, ch 1, 1 d c in each d c, repeat from * 4 times, double picot loop and sl st in ch 3 to join.

4th Row. Ch 3, 3 d c in center d c, 1 d c in last d c, * double picot loop, 1 d c in 1st d c, 3 d c in center d c, 1 d c in last d c, repeat from * 4 times, double picot loop and sl st in 3 ch loop to join.

5th Row. Ch 3, 1 d c in next d c, 3 d c in center d c, 1 d c in each of the next 2 d c, * ch 7, 1 d c in each of the next 2 d c, 3 d c in center d c, 1 d c in each of the next 2 d c, repeat from * 4 times, ch 7, join in 3 ch loop.

6th Row. Ch 1, 1 s c in each d c and 5 s c, ch 4, 5 s c over each loop.

7th Row. Ch 10, skip 5 s c, s c in next s c, ch 10, skip 10 s c of scallop, s c in next s c, repeat from beginning all around.

8th Row. Sl st to loop, ch 1, * 1 s c and 5 d c over loop, ch 5, 5 d c and 1 s c over same loop, s c in next s c, ch 6, tr c over next loop, ch 6, s c in next s c and repeat from * all around.

9th Row. Sl st to 3rd d c of petal, * ch 9, s c in 3rd d c on other side of petal, ch 6, d c in tr c, ch 3, tr c in same space, ch 3, d c in same space, ch 6, s c in 3rd st of next petal and repeat from * all around.

10th Row. 1 s c and 5 d c over next loop, ch 5, 5 d c and 1 s c over same loop, ch 5, d c in next d c, ch 5, tr c in tr c, ch 5, tr c in same space, ch 5, d c in next d c, ch 5 and repeat from beginning all around joining row in s c of 1st petal.

Join motifs in the last row as follows, work 1 petal, ch 5, d c in d c, ch 5, tr c in tr c, ch 2, slip loop off hook, insert in center of corresponding loop of 1st motif and pull loop through (all joinings are made in same manner), ch 2, tr c in tr c of second motif, ch 5, d c in d c, ch 5, 1 s c and 5 d c over loop, ch 2, join to corresponding picot of 1st motif, ch 2, 5 d c and 1 s c over remainder of loop, ch 5, d c in next d c, ch 5, tr c in tr c, ch 2, join to corresponding loop of 1st motif, ch 2 and complete row. Join all motifs in same manner.

DOILY No. 2204

Materials Required—AMERICAN THREAD COMPANY "STAR" or "GEM" MERCERIZED CROCHET COTTON, Size 20 or 30

1—300 Yd. Ball White, Ecru or Colors.
Steel Crochet Hook No. 11 or 12.
Each Motif measures about 3 inches. Doily 3 x 5 Motifs measured about 9 x 15 inches.

Motif. Ch 8, join, ch 5, tr c into ring, * ch 2, tr c into ring, repeat from * 9 times, ch 2, sl st into 3rd st of ch to join (12 meshes).

2nd Row. Ch 1, 3 s c in each mesh, join.

3rd Row. Ch 1, s c in each s c taking up back loop of st only, join.

4th Row. Ch 4, d c in next s c taking up back loop of st only, * ch 1, d c in next s c taking up back loop of st only, repeat from * all around, join in 3rd st of ch.

5th Row. Ch 1, 2 s c in each mesh (72 s c), join.

6th Row. Ch 4, 1 tr c in each of the next 4 s c, * ch 7, skip 1 s c, 1 tr c in each of the next 5 s c, repeat from * 10 times, ch 7, join.

7th Row. Ch 1, 1 s c in each tr c and 4 s c, ch 4, 4 s c in each loop, join.

8th Row. Sl st to center s c, ch 1, s c in same space, * ch 7, d c in next picot, ch 3, d c in same picot, ch 7, s c in center s c, repeat from * all around.

Motifs are joined together in the last row. Work to within the last 2 points, * d c into picot, ch 1, sl st into shell of 1st motif, ch 1, d c into same picot of 2nd motif, ch 7, s c into center s c, ch 7, repeat from *. Join 3rd motif to 2nd motif and 4th motif to 1st and 3rd motif.

Joining Motif. Fasten thread in 3 ch loop, ch 6, d c in same space, ch 5, tr c between motifs, ch 5, d c in next 3 ch space, ch 3, d c in same space and continue around joining in 4th st of ch 6.

2nd Row. Ch 4, 1 d c in same space, ch 3, 2 d c in same space, 2 d c, ch 3, 2 d c in next 3 ch space, repeat twice. Join and break thread.

DOILY No. 2205

Materials Required—AMERICAN THREAD COMPANY "STAR" or "GEM" MERCERIZED CROCHET COTTON, Size 30

1—300 Yd. Ball White or Colors.
Steel Crochet Hook No. 11 or 12.
Each Motif measures about 3½ inches. 7 Motifs are required for doily illustrated which measures about 10 inches through the center.

Motif. Ch 11, join to form a ring and work 24 s c in ring, join.

Continued on page 78

Picot Picot

Materials Required:
AMERICAN THREAD COMPANY
The Famous "PURITAN" MERCERIZED
   CROCHET COTTON, Article 40
1 ball Yellow or
The Famous "PURITAN" STAR SPANGLED
   MERCERIZED CROCHET COTTON, Article 40
2 balls Yellow Spangle or color of your choice
Steel Crochet Hook No. 7
App size: 11½ inches in diameter for "PURITAN";
   12½ inches in diameter for "PURITAN" STAR
   SPANGLED

Chain (ch) 7, slip stitch (sl st) in 5th st from hook for picot, ch 7, sl st in 7th st from hook for picot, ch 5, sl st in 5th st from hook for picot, sl st in 1st picot (3 picot group), repeat from beginning 5 times, join in 1st st of ch. 2nd ROUND: Ch 15, treble treble crochet (tr trc: 4 times over hook) in same space, * ch 10, 2 tr trc with ch 10 between each tr trc in space between next 3 picot groups, repeat from * 4 times, ch 10, join in 6th st of ch. 3rd ROUND: 5 single crochet (sc), ch 5, 5 sc in each loop, join in 1st sc. 4th ROUND: Sl st to next ch 5 loop, ch 9, * double treble crochet (d trc: 3 times over hook) in same space, ch 5, repeat from * once, tr trc in same space, * ch 5, d trc in same space, repeat from * twice, ch 2, 3 sc in next loop, ch 2, d trc in next loop, ch 5, repeat from 1st * all around ending to correspond, join in 5th st of ch. 5th ROUND: Ch 1, sc in same space, * 4 sc in next loop, sc in next st, repeat from * 5 times, working over sc and into ch 5 loop of 3rd round, 3 double crochet (dc) in loop, sc in next st, repeat from 1st * all around ending to correspond, join in 1st sc. 6th ROUND: Ch 3, dc in same space, * ch 4, skip 4 sc, 2 d trc in next sc, repeat from * once, ch 4, skip 4 sc, 2 d trc, ch 4, 2 d trc, ch 4, 2 d trc in next sc, * ch 4, skip 4 sc, 2 d trc in next sc, repeat from * once, ch 4, skip 4 sc, 2 dc in next sc, 2 dc in next sc, repeat from 1st * all around ending to correspond, join in 3rd st of ch. 7th ROUND: Sl st to next loop, ch 1, 3 sc in same loop, sc in each of the next 2 d trc, * 3 sc in the next loop, 1 sc in each of the next 2 d trc, repeat from * 5 times, 3 sc in next loop, skip next dc, * thread over, insert hook in next dc, pull thread through, repeat from * once, thread over and work off all loops at one time, repeat from 1st * all around ending to correspond, join in 1st sc. 8th ROUND: Sl st over next 3 sc, ch 5, d trc in next sc, * ch 2, skip 3 sc, 2 d trc in each of the next 2 sc, repeat from * once, ch 2, skip 3 sc, * 4 d trc in next sc, ch 3, 4 d trc in next sc, ch 2, * skip 3 sc, 2 d trc in each of the next 2 sc, ch 2, repeat from * once, skip 3 sc, 1 d trc in each of the next 2 sc, skip 7 sts, 1 d trc in each of

Continued on page 79

70

Sea Spray

MATERIALS:

J. & P. COATS or CLARK'S O.N.T. BEST SIX CORD MERCERIZED CROCHET, Size 30:

SMALL BALL:

J. & P. COATS —2 balls of White or Ecru, or 3 balls of any color,

or

CLARK'S O.N.T.—4 balls of White, Ecru or any color.

Steel Crochet Hook No. 10 or 11.

This amount is sufficient for a set consisting of 1 large doily about 10 x 15 inches and 2 small doilies each about 10 inches in diameter.

Small Doily (Make 2) . . . Starting at center ch 10. Join with sl st to form ring. **1st rnd:** Ch 1, 16 sc in ring. Sl st in 1st sc made. **2nd rnd:** Ch 4 (to count as 1 tr), tr in same place as sl st, 2 tr in each sc around (32 tr). Sl st in top st of starting chain. **3rd rnd:** Ch 4, holding back the last loop of each tr on hook, make tr in next 2 sts, thread over and draw through all loops on hook (3-tr cluster made); * ch 9, holding back the last loop of each tr on hook make tr in same place as last tr, tr in each of next 2 sts, complete a 3-tr cluster as before. Repeat from * around. Join last ch-9 with sl st in tip of 1st cluster. **4th rnd:** Sl st to center of loop, ch 13, * in center st of next loop make tr, ch 5, sc in 4th ch from hook (p made), ch 1 and tr, ch 9. Repeat from * around, ending with ch 1, p, ch 1, sl st in 4th st of ch-13. **5th rnd:** Sl st to center

Continued on page 80

Scroll Doily

Materials Required — AMERICAN THREAD COM-PANY "STAR" MERCERIZED CROCHET COTTON, Article 30, Size 50.

1—150 yd. Ball White.
Steel Crochet Hook No. 13.
Doily measures about 9¼ inches.

Ch 6, join to form a ring, ch 5, d c in ring, * ch 2, d c in ring, repeat from * 5 times, ch 2, join in 3rd st of ch.

2nd Row. Ch 1 and work 2 s c over each 2 ch mesh.

3rd Row. Ch 5, d c in next s c, * ch 2, d c in next s c, repeat from * all around, ch 2, join in 3rd st of ch (16 d c).

4th Row. Ch 1 and work 3 s c over each 2 ch mesh.

5th Row. Ch 18, s c in 2nd st from hook and work 19 s c over balance of ch, sl st in next 2 s c of center, ** ch 1, turn, work in back loop of st only for entire scroll, 1 s c in each of the next 19 s c on scroll, ch 3, turn, skip 2 sts of ch, 1 s c in next st of ch, 1 s c in each of the next 5 s c, * ch 1, turn, 1 s c in each of the next 4 s c, ch 3, turn, skip 2 sts of ch, 1 s c in next st of ch, 1 s c in each of the next 4 s c, 1 s c in each of the next 2 s c on base of scroll, repeat from * 6 times, sl st in next 4 s c of center, ch 17, turn, s c in 3rd picot from bottom of scroll just completed, ch 1, turn, and work 20 s c over ch, sl st in each of the next 2 s c of center, repeat from ** until 7

scrolls are completed. Work another scroll joining it to 1st scroll in the 6th picot, complete scroll, then sl st in each of the next 4 s c of center, break thread.

Attach thread in 2nd free picot of any scroll, s c in same space, ** ch 5, s c in next free picot, * ch 5, s c in next free picot, repeat from *, ch 5, skip 1st picot of next scroll, s c in next free picot, repeat from ** 6 times ending row with * ch 5, s c in next picot, repeat from * twice, ch 3, d c in 1st s c, this brings thread in position for next row.

2nd Row. S c in same space, ch 3, s c in same space, * ch 6, s c in next loop, ch 3, s c in same space, repeat from * all around ending row with ch 3, d c in first s c.

3rd, 4th & 5th Rows. S c in same space, ch 3, s c in same space, * ch 6, s c in next 6 ch loop, ch 3, s c in same space, repeat from * all around ending each row same as last row.

6th Row. S c in same space, ch 3, s c in same space, ** ch 6, cluster st in next loop, (cluster st: thread over needle twice, insert in loop and work off 2 loops twice, * thread over needle twice, insert in same space and work off 2 loops twice, repeat from *, thread over and work off re-maining loops at one time) ch 4, sl st in top of cluster st for picot, ch 3, cluster st in same loop, picot, ch 3, cluster st in same loop, picot, ch 6, s c in next loop, ch 3, s c in same loop, repeat from ** all around ending row with

Continued on page 79

Floral Garland Doily

ROYAL SOCIETY SIX CORD CORDICHET,
Size 30, 2 balls of White or Ecru.

Steel Crochet Hook No. 10.

Piece of linen 6 inches in diameter.

Doily measures 13½ inches in diameter.

Roll edge of linen and baste. **1st rnd:** Make 272 sc around rolled edge. **2nd rnd:** Ch 3, dc in next 15 sc, * (ch 5, skip 2 sc, sc in next sc) 5 times; ch 5, skip 3 sc, dc in next 16 sc. Repeat from * around. Join with sl st. **3rd rnd:** Sl st in next 2 dc, ch 3, dc in next 11 dc, * (ch 5, sc in next loop) 6 times; ch 5, skip 2 dc, dc in next 12 dc. Repeat from * around. Join. **4th rnd:** Sl st in next 2 dc, ch 4, tr in next 7 dc, * (ch 5, sc in next loop) 7 times; ch 5, skip 2 dc, tr in next 8 dc. Repeat from * around. Join. **5th rnd:** Ch 4, holding back on hook the last loop of each tr make tr in next 3 tr, thread over and draw through all loops on hook (cluster made), * ch 3, 4-tr cluster over next 4 tr, (ch 5, sc in next loop) 8 times; ch 5, cluster over next 4 tr. Repeat from * around. Join. **6th rnd:** Sl st in next loop, ch 6, dc in next loop, * (ch 5, tr in next loop) 7 times; ch 5, dc in next loop, (ch 3, dc in next loop) twice. Repeat from * around. Join to 3rd ch of ch-6. **7th rnd:** Ch 6, dc in next dc, * (ch 5, tr in tr) twice; ch 5, sc in next tr, ch 5, 5-d tr cluster in same tr, skip next tr, 5-d tr cluster in next tr, ch 5, sl st at base of cluster, (ch 5, tr in next tr) twice; ch 5, dc in next dc, (ch 3, dc in next dc) twice. Repeat from * around. Join. **8th rnd:** Ch 6, * dc in next dc, ch 5, tr in next tr, ch 7, d tr in next tr, 6-d tr cluster in center of previous 2 clusters, (ch 9, 6-d tr cluster in same place) twice; d tr in next tr, ch 7, tr in next tr, ch 5, dc in next dc, ch 3, dc in next dc, ch 3. Repeat from * around. Join. **9th rnd:** * Ch 7, skip ch-3 sp, tr in next sp, ch 5, d tr in next sp, (ch 5, in next sp make tr, ch 5 and tr) twice; ch 5, d tr in next

sp, ch 5, tr in next sp, ch 7, skip 1 dc, sc in next dc. Repeat from * around. Join. **10th rnd:** * 9 sc in next loop, 7 sc in next 7 loops, 9 sc in next loop. Repeat from * around. Join. **11th rnd:** Sl st in next 2 sc, sc in next sc, * (ch 3, skip 1 sc, sc in next sc) 31 times; ch 3, skip 4 sc, sc in next sc. Repeat from * around, ending with ch 3. Join. **12th rnd:** Sl st across first loop, * (sc in next loop, ch 3) 28 times; sc in next loop, ch 5, skip 3 loops. Repeat from * around, ending with ch 2, dc in first sc. **13th rnd:** * Ch 5, skip 1 loop, (sc in next loop, ch 3) 25 times; sc in next loop, ch 5, skip 1 loop, sc in next loop. Repeat from * around, ending with ch 2, dc in dc. **14th rnd:** Ch 7, sc in next loop, ch 7, skip 1 loop, sc in next loop, * (ch 3, sc in next loop) 22 times; ch 7, skip 1 loop, sc in

Continued on page 80

Entertaining Ideas

MATERIALS—DAISY Mercerized Crochet Cotton, size 30 in White, Cream or Ecru. 1 skein or ball is sufficient for 4 doilies. Crochet hook size 13. Sizes—6½ to 7 inches.

A—DOILY—"WHIRL AROUND" (Center of photograph)

Ch 8, sl st in 1st st. Ch 7, tr in ring, (ch 1, tr) 16 times in ring, ch 1, sl st in 6th st of 1st 7-ch. **ROW 2**—Ch 3, (2 dc in next 1-ch sp, 1 dc in tr) repeated around, sl st in 1st 3-ch. **ROW 3**—(Ch 25, sc in next 3d dc) 18 times. Cut 6 inches long, thread to a needle and fasten off on back. **ROW 4**—Sl st in 13th st of one lp, ch 7, tr in same st, (ch 2, tr) twice in same st, * tr in 13th st of next lp, (ch 2, tr) 3 times in same st. Repeat from * around, sl st in 5th st of 1st 7-ch. **ROW 5**—Ch 1, * (1 sc, 1 hdc and 1 dc) in next 2-ch sp, dc in tr, 3 dc in next sp, dc in tr, (1 dc, 1 hdc and 1 sc) in next sp, sc between shells. Repeat from * around. Sl st up to center of 1st shell. **ROW 6**—Ch 11, * (dc, ch 3, dc) in center st of next shell, ch 8. Repeat from * around. Join final 3-ch to 3d st of 1st 11-ch. **ROW 7**—Ch 4, turn, dc in 3-ch sp, (ch 1, dc) twice in same sp, * ch 7, dc in next shell, (ch 1, dc) 3 times in same shell. Repeat from * around. Join final 7-ch to 3d st of 1st 4-ch. **ROW 8**—Ch 9, turn, * dc in next dc, (ch 2, dc in next dc) 3 times, ch 6. Repeat from * around. Join final 2-ch to 3d st of 1st 9-ch. **ROW 9**—Ch 3, turn, dc in same st, * (ch 2, 2 dc in next dc) 3 times, ch 4, 2 dc in next dc. Repeat from * around and join to 1st 3-ch. **ROW 10**—Ch 6, turn, * dc in next 2 dc, (ch 2, dc in next 2 dc) 3 times, ch 3. Repeat from * around. End with 1 dc, sl st in 3d st of 1st 6-ch. **ROW 11**—Ch 3, turn, * 2 dc in next dc, (ch 2, dc in next dc, 2 dc in next dc) 3 times, dc in next dc. Repeat from * around and join to 1st 3-ch. **ROW 12**—Ch 1, turn, sc in next dc, * hdc in next, (ch 2, dc in next dc, 2 dc in next, 1 dc in next) twice, ch 2, hdc in next dc, sc in next 4 dc. Repeat from * around. Cut 6 inches long, thread to a needle and fasten off on back.

B—DOILY—"LIGHT AND AIRY" (Upper right)

Ch 8, sl st in 1st st. (Ch 35, sc in ring) 8 times. Cut 6 inches long, thread to a needle and fasten off on back. **ROW 2**—10 sc across center of 1 lp, (ch 3, 10 sc in next lp) 7 times, ch 3, sl st in 1st sc. **ROW 3**—* Ch 7, sk last ch st, 6 sc on ch, sl st in next sc. Ch 1, turn, sk sl st and in back lps only, sc in last 5 sc, ch 4, turn, sk last ch st, 3 sc on ch, sc in 5 sc, sl st in next sc on center. Ch 1, turn, sk sl st, sc in next 7 sc, ch 4, turn, 3 sc on ch, 7 sc, sl st in next 2d sc. Ch 1, turn, 9 sc, ch 4, turn, 3 sc on ch, 9 sc, sl st in next 2d sc. Ch 1, turn, 9 sc, ch 2, turn, 1 sc on ch, 9 sc, sl st in next sc. Ch 1, turn, 7 sc, ch 2, turn, 1 sc on ch, 7 sc, sl st in next sc. Ch 1, turn, 5 sc, ch 2, turn, 1 sc on ch, 5 sc, sl st in end sc, 3 sc in next 3-ch sp, sl st in next sc. Repeat from * around. Fasten off on back. **ROW 4**—Join to center of 1 point, * ch 12, dtr in end of next 2d rib, dtr in 2d rib of next point, ch 12, sc in center of same point. Repeat from * around. **ROW 5**—* (Ch 8, tr tr) twice in next dtr. Repeat from * once. Ch 8, sc in next sc. Repeat from * around. **ROW 6**—(10 sc in next 8-ch sp, sc in tr tr) twice, * (5 sc, ch 5, sl st in last sc for a p, and 5 sc) in next sp, sc in tr tr, 10 sc in next sp, sc in tr tr, 10 sc in next 2 sps, sc in tr tr, ch 7, turn, sl st back in 11th sc up side of previous shell, ch 1, turn, (1 sc, 1 hdc, 7 dc, 1 hdc and 1 sc) all in 6-ch lp, 5 sc in half of next sp, ch 2, turn, tr in 3d st on added lp, (ch 2, tr in next st) 6 times, ch 2, sl st in next 5th sc on shell, ch 1, turn, 3 sc in next 2-ch sp, (2 sc, a p and 2 sc in next sp) 6 times, 3 sc in next sp, 5 sc in next sp, 1 sc in tr tr. Repeat from * around. Sl st in 1st 11 sc and make added shell. Fasten off on back.

C—DOILY—"LATTICED AND LOVELY" (Lower right)

Ch 8, sl st in 1st st. Ch 3, 19 dc in ring, sl st in 1st 3-ch. **ROW 2**—(Ch 1 and in back lps only, 3 dc in next dc, ch 1, sc in next dc) 10 times. Sl st to center dc of next scallop. **ROW 3**—Ch 4, (dc, ch 1, dc) in same st, (ch 1, dc) 3 times in center dc of each scallop around. Ch 1, sl st in 3d st of 1st 4-ch. **ROW 4**—Ch 6, turn, * dc in next dc, (ch 1, dc in next dc) twice, ch 3 and repeat from * around. Join final 1-ch to 3d st of 1st 6-ch. **ROW 5**—Ch 4, turn, dc in next dc, ch 1, dc in next dc, * ch 5, dc in next dc, (ch 1, dc in next dc) twice. Repeat from * around. Join final 5-ch to 3d st of 1st 4-ch. **ROW 6**—Ch 10, turn, * dc in next dc, (ch 1, dc in next dc) twice, ch 7. Repeat from * around and join final 1-ch to 3d st of 1st 10-ch. **ROW 7**—Ch 3, turn, (dc in next 2 dc, holding back the last lp of each dc, thread over and pull thru all lps at once (a Cluster made), * ch 13, (dc in next 3 dc) made into a Cluster. Repeat from * around and join to 1st Cluster. **ROW 8**—Ch 3, turn, (14 dc in next sp, 1 dc in Cluster) repeated around and join to 3-ch, sl st in next dc. **ROW 9**—Ch 4, dc in next 2d dc, ch 1, dc in next 2d dc, * ch 9, dc in next 5th dc, (ch 1, dc in next 2d dc) 5 times. Repeat from * around. Join final 1-ch to 3d st of 1st 4-ch. **ROW 10**—Ch 4, turn, dc in next dc, (ch 1, dc in next dc) twice, * ch 9, dc in next dc, (ch 1, dc in next dc) 5 times. Repeat from * around. Join final 1-ch to 3d st of 1st 4-ch. **ROW 11**—Ch 4, turn, dc in next dc, ch 1, dc in next dc, * ch 6, sc under center of next 2 lps, ch 6, dc in next dc, (ch 1, dc in next dc) 5 times. Repeat from * around and join. **ROW 12**—Repeat Row 10 to *. ** Ch 1, dc in next 6-ch lp, ch 10, dc in next lp, (ch 1, dc in next dc) 6 times. Repeat from ** around and join. **ROW 13**—Ch 4, turn, dc in next dc, (ch 1, dc in next dc) twice, * ch 10, dc in next dc, (ch 1, dc in next dc) 7 times. Repeat from * around and join. **ROW 14**—Ch 4, turn, dc in next dc, (ch 1, dc in next dc) 3 times, * ch 6, sc under center of next 2 lps, ch 6, dc in next dc, (ch 1, dc in next dc) 7 times. Repeat from * around and join. **ROW 15**—Ch 11, turn, dtr in next dc, ch 3, dtr in next dc, * ch 3, tr in next dc, ch 6, sc in next sc, ch 6, tr in next dc, (ch 3, dtr in next dc) twice, (ch 3, tr tr in next dc) twice, (ch 3, dtr in next dc) twice. Repeat from * around. Join final 3-ch to 8th st of 1st 11-ch. **ROW 16**—(Sc, ch 1, 3 dc, ch 1, sc) in each 3-ch sp around, 6 sc in each 6-ch sp. Cut 6 inches long, thread to a needle and fasten off on back.

Continued on page 75

Frost Flower Refreshment Set

MATERIALS—Lily Sil-Tone Mercerized Crochet Cotton:—4 balls White (100-yd. balls) —sufficient for Doily and 4 Coasters. Crochet hook size 12.

MOTIF—Ch 6, sl st in 1st st. Ch 5, dc in ring, (ch 2, dc in ring) 6 times, ch 2, sl st in 3d st of 1st 5-ch. **ROW 2**—(Sc, ch 1, 3 dc, ch 1 and sc) in each 2-ch sp. **ROW 3**— Sl st to center dc of 1st petal, ch 3 for a dc, (ch 8, sl st in 1 lp of 5th ch st from hook for a p, ch 4, dc in next petal) 7 times, ch 8, p, ch 4, sl st in 3d st of 1st lp. **ROW 4**— Ch 3, turn, 2 dc in same st with sl st, (ch 8, p, ch 4, 3 dc in next dc) 7 times, ch 8, p, ch 4, sl st in 1st 3-ch. **ROW 5**—Ch 3 for a dc, turn, (ch 7, p, ch 3, 2 dc in each dc) repeated around. End with 5 dc, sl st in 3d st of 1st lp. **ROW 6**—Ch 3, turn, dc in sl st, 2 dc in next dc, * dc in next 2 dc, (2 dc in next dc) twice, ch 7, (2 dc in next dc) twice. Repeat from * around and join to 1st 3-ch. **ROW 7**—Ch 3, turn, sc in center of last 7-ch lp, * (2 dc in next dc) twice, (1 dc in next dc, 2 dc in next) 4 times, sc in center of next lp. Repeat from * around. End with 1 less dc, sl st in 1st dc, sl st in next sc. **ROW 8**—Turn, * ch 2, dc in next 2d dc, ch 2, tr in next 2d dc, (ch 2, dtr in next 2d dc) twice, ch 2, dtr in next dc, ch 2, dtr in next 2d dc, ch 2, tr in next 2d dc, ch 2, dc in next 2d st, ch 2, sc in sc between fans. Repeat from * 7 times. **ROW 9**—Ch 1, turn, * 2 sc in next sp, 3 sc in next, (2 sc, ch 5, sl st in last sc for a p, and 2 sc —all in next sp) 5 times, 3 sc in next sp, 2 sc in next. Repeat from * 7 times. Cut 6 inches long, thread to a needle and fasten off on back.

Make a Motif for each Coaster.

DOILY—Make 8 Motifs and join into a circle by 2 shells on each side of each, joining by the last 3 ps on one shell and the 1st 3 ps on next. Leave one shell free between joinings on inside of circle. To join ps, instead of a 5-ch p, make 2-ch, sl st in corresponding p on adjoining Motif, ch 2 back, sl st in last sc to complete p. Repeat with each joining.

Center—Make another Motif. Join to center p on a shell, * ch 9, p, ch 10, p, ch 5, tr in next 2d p, tr in 1st p on next shell, ch 9, p, ch 10, p, ch 5, sc in next 2d p. Repeat from * around and fasten off. **ROW 2**— Join to center of last p-lp, * ch 10, p, ch 3, sl st in center p of free shell on one Motif in circle, ch 3, tr at base of last p, ch 5, sl st in tr for a p, ch 6, sc in next lp, (ch 10, p) twice, ch 5, sl st in 1st p on next shell of same Motif, ch 5, dc back at base of last p, ch 6, p, ch 7, sl st in 2d p on next shell on next Motif, ch 5, dc back in 6th st of 7-ch, a p, ch 2, tr in center st between 1st 2 ps at start of this p-lp, ch 7, p, ch 6, sc in next p-lp of last row. Repeat from * 7 times to complete circle. Fasten off.

Stretch and pin right-side-down in true circles. Steam and press dry thru a cloth.

Entertaining Ideas

Continued from page 74

D—DOILY—"DANCING FANS" (Lower left)

Ch 10, tr in 1st st, (ch 4, tr in same st) 6 times, ch 4, sl st in next 5th ch st. **ROW 2**—Ch 1, (5 sc in next sp, sc in tr) repeated around, sl st in 1st 1-ch. **ROW 3**—* Ch 4, (dc, ch 4, dc) in next 3d sc, ch 4, sc in next 3d sc. Repeat from * 7 times. **ROW 4**—(4 sc in next sp, 5 sc in next, 4 sc in next) 8 times. Sl st up to center sc of next shell. **ROW 5**—(Ch 9, sc in 2 lps of 5th st from hook for a p, ch 12, p, ch 5, sc in same point) 8 times. Cut 6 inches long, thread to a needle and fasten off on back. **ROW 6**— Join to center of 1 lp, (ch 10, p, ch 14, p, ch 6, sc in next lp) 8 times. Fasten off as before. **ROW 7**—Join to center st of 1 lp, * ch 3, 7 dc in same st. Ch 5, turn, sk last dc, dc in next dc, (ch 2, dc in next st) 6 times. Ch 6, turn, dc in next dc, (ch 3, dc in next dc) 5 times, ch 3, dc in 3d st of end 5-ch. Ch 8, turn, dc in next dc, (ch 5, dc in next dc) 5 times, ch 5, dc in 4th st of end 6-ch. * Cut 3 inches long. ** Turn, join to center st of next lp to left of last Fan and repeat from * to *. Ch 2, sl st in corner of last Fan and cut 3 inches long. Repeat from ** around. Join 1st and last Fans. **Edge**—Make 7 sc in center sp of one Fan, (7 sc in next sp) 3 times, * 1 sc between Fans, 7 sc in next sp, 4 sc in half of next sp, ch 16, turn, sl st back in center of 2d sp up side of last Fan, ch 1, turn, 1 sc in lp, (1 hdc, 5 dc, 1 hdc and 1 sc) 3 times in lp, 3 sc in bal. of sp on Fan, 4 sc in next sp, turn, (ch 10, sc in next scallop) 3 times, ch 10, sl st in center of next sp on Fan. Ch 1, turn, (6 sc, ch 5, sl st in last sc for a p, and 6 sc) in each 10-ch lp, 3 sc in bal. of sp on Fan, (7 sc in next sp) 4 times. Repeat from * around, working over ends left from Fans. Fasten off as before.

Stretch and pin each Doily right-side-down in a true circle. Steam and press dry thru a cloth.

Victoriana

MATERIALS:

CLARK'S BIG BALL MERCERIZED CROCHET, Art. B.34, Size 30: 1 ball each of No. 181 Shaded Lt. Yellows and No. 76 Robinette; or

J. & P. Coats Best Six Cord Mercerized Crochet, Art. A.104, Size 30: 1 ball each of No. 181 Shaded Lt. Yellows and a color of your own choice.

Milwards Steel Crochet Hook No. 10.

A piece of aqua linen about 9 inches square.

Doily measures 17½ inches in diameter.

BRAIDED SECTION . . . Starting at inner edge with Shaded Lt. Yellows, ch 6, in 6th ch from hook make dc, ch 2 and dc (shell made); ch 5, turn; (in sp of shell just made, make dc, ch 2 and dc—shell made over shell—ch 5, turn) 10 times; shell over shell, * ch 2, insert hook through previous 3 loops on same side, thread over and complete as a sl st, thus forming a scallop, ch 2, turn; (shell over shell, ch 5, turn, shell over shell, ch 2, sl st in adjacent free loop opposite, ch 2, turn) 3 times; (shell over shell, ch 5, turn) 6 times; shell over shell, ch 2, sl st through previous 3 loops to form scallop as before, ch 2, turn. Continue making braid, joining 4 loops on one side to adjacent loops opposite. Continue making braid until there are 4 free ch-5 loops on same side as last joining, ending with shell over shell, ch 2, sl st through previous 3 loops to form scallop, ch 2, turn and continue making braid, joining 6 loops with loops opposite, ending with shell over shell; make braid until there are 2 free loops on same side as last joining, ending with shell over shell, ch 2, form scallop as before, ch 2, turn. Make braid, joining 4 loops to loops opposite, ending with shell over shell. Work braid until there are 2 free loops have been completed on same side as last joining, ending with shell over shell. Repeat from * around, until there are 34 scallops on both inner and outer edges, ending with ch 2, turn; dc in sp of last shell made, ch 1, sl st at base of

Continued on page 80

Chariot Wheels

DOILY No. 2212

Materials Required—AMERICAN THREAD COMPANY "STAR" or "GEM" MERCERIZED CROCHET COTTON, Size 20 or 30

2—300 Yd. Balls White or Colors.
Steel Crochet Hook No. 11 or 12.
Doily measures 15 inches at the widest point.

Ch 5, join to form a ring, ch 7, 1 d c in ring, * ch 4, 1 d c in ring, repeat from * 3 times, ch 4, join to 3rd st of ch.

2nd Row. Ch 5, 6 d c in 1st space, * ch 2, 6 d c in next space, repeat from * all around working 5 d c in last space, join to 3rd st of ch.

3rd Row. Ch 4, 5 tr c in 1st space, * ch 6, 6 tr c in next space, repeat from * all around, ch 6 and join.

4th Row. Ch 4, 1 tr c in each tr c, * ch 5, 1 s c in center of ch 6, ch 5, tr c in each tr c, repeat from * all around. Work 36 more motifs and sew them together as follows: 4 in the 1st row, 5 in the 2nd row, 6 in the 3rd row and 7 in the 4th row, which is the center, continue, having one less motif in each row until there are 4 motifs in row.

Edge: Join thread to ch 5 at point, ch 9, * s c in 1st st of next ch 5, ch 7, skip 4 sts of next loop, s c in next st, ch 7, s c in 1st st of next loop, ch 7, skip 2 loops and 4 sts of next loop, s c in next st, ch 7, repeat from * all around.

2nd Row. Sl st in loop, ch 3, 11 d c in same loop, (ch 3 counts as 1 d c) ch 5, s c in next loop, ch 5, s c in next loop, ch 5, 12 d c in large loop, ch 5, s c in next loop, ch 5, s c in next loop, ch 5, s c in next loop, ch 5, 12 d c in next loop and continue all around.

3rd Row. Ch 3, 1 d c with 1 ch between in every d c, ch 2, s c in next loop, ch 5, s c in next loop, ch 5, s c in next loop, ch 2, d c with 1 ch between in every d c and continue all around.

4th Row. Ch 3, d c in d c, * ch 4, sl st in top of d c just made for picot, ch 1, d c in top of d c, repeat from * 10 times, d c in d c, ch 2, s c in 5 ch loop, s c in next loop, ch 2, * d c in top of d c, ch 4, sl st in top of d c just made for picot, repeat from * 10 times, d c in d c, ch 2, s c in next 5 ch loop, s c in next loop, s c in next loop, ch 2 and continue all around.

Rock Pool

Continued from page 66

hook out to measure ¼ inch, thread over and draw loop through, insert hook between single and double loops and draw loop through, thread over and draw through all loops on hook (knot st made), dc in next picot, make a knot st, (picot in next shell, shell in next picot) 5 times. Repeat from * around. Join. **25th rnd:** Sl st to center dc of shell, picot in same place, (shell in next picot, picot in next shell) twice; * make a knot st, dc in next picot, make a knot st, sc under double loop of next knot st, sc in next dc, sc in next knot st, make a knot st, dc in next loop, make a knot st, (picot in next shell, shell in next picot) 4 times; picot in next shell. Repeat from * around. Join.

26th rnd: (Shell in next picot, picot in next shell) twice; * make a knot st, dc in next loop, make a knot st, sc in next knot st, in next dc and in next knot st, make a knot st, dc in center sc of next group, make a knot st, sc in next knot st, next dc and next knot st, make a knot st, dc in next picot, make a knot st, (picot in next shell, shell in next picot) 3 times; picot in next shell. Repeat from * around. Join. **27th rnd:** Sl st to center dc of next shell, picot in same place, shell in next picot, * picot in next shell, make a knot st, dc in next picot, (make a knot st, sc in next knot st, next dc and next knot st, make a knot st, dc in center sc of next group) twice; make a knot st, sc in next knot st, next dc and next knot st, make a knot st, dc in next picot, make a knot st, (picot in next shell, shell in next picot) twice. Repeat from * around. Join. **28th rnd:** Sl st in next picot, shell in same place, * picot in next shell, make a knot st, dc in next picot, (make a knot st, sc in next knot st, in next dc and next knot st, make a knot st, dc in center sc of next 3-sc group) 3 times; make a knot st, sc in next knot st, in next dc and in next knot st, make a knot st, dc in

next picot, make a knot st, picot in next shell, shell in next picot. Repeat from * around. Join.

29th rnd: Sl st to center of next shell, picot in same place, * make a knot st, dc in next picot, (make a knot st, sc in next knot st, next dc and in next knot st, make a knot st, dc in center sc of next sc group) 4 times; make a knot st, sc in next knot st, in next dc and next knot st, make a knot st, dc in next picot, make a knot st, picot in next shell. Repeat from * around. Join. **30th rnd:** Sl st in next picot, ch 3, * (make a knot st, sc in next knot st, next dc and next knot st, make a knot st, dc in center sc of next sc group) 5 times; make a knot st, sc in next knot st, in next dc and in next knot st, make a knot st, dc in next picot. Repeat from * around. Join to top of ch-3. **31st rnd:** Sc in same place as sl st, sc in next knot st, * make a knot st, sc in next knot st, in next dc and in next knot st, make a knot st, dc in center sc of next sc group. Repeat from * around, ending with sc in last knot st. Join. **32nd rnd:** Ch 3, * make a knot st, sc in next knot st, in next dc and in next knot st, make a knot st, dc in center sc of next sc group. Repeat from * around. Join to top of ch-3. **33rd rnd:** Sc in same place as sl st, * ch 7, sc in next dc, ch 7, dc in center sc of next sc group. Repeat from * around. Join.

RUFFLE . . . 1st rnd: 8 sc in each sp around. Join. **2nd rnd:** Sc in same place as sl st, * ch 5, skip next sc, sc in next sc. Repeat from * around, ending with ch 2, dc in first sc. **3rd to 7th rnds incl:** * Ch 5, sc in next loop. Repeat from * around, ending with ch 2, dc in dc. **8th rnd:** * Ch 6, sc in next loop. Repeat from * around, ending with ch 3, dc in dc. **9th rnd:** * Ch 7, sc in next loop. Repeat from * around, ending with ch 3, tr in dc. **10th rnd:** * Ch 8, sc in next loop. Repeat from * around, ending with ch 4, tr in tr. **11th to 14th rnds incl:** * Ch 9, sc in next loop. Repeat from * around, ending with ch 5, tr in tr. At end of 14th rnd, ch 9, sl st in tr. Break off. Starch lightly and press.

Three's Company

Continued from page 69

2nd Row. Ch 4, cluster st in same st. (To make cluster st, counting the ch 4 as 1 tr c, thread over needle twice, insert in st, pull loop through, thread over and pull through 2 loops, thread over and pull through next 2 loops, thread over needle twice, insert in same st, pull through, thread over and pull through 2 loops, thread over and pull through next 2 loops, thread over and pull through all loops on needle.) * Ch 7, skip 1 s c, 3 tr c cluster st in next s c and repeat from * all around, ch 7, join to top of 1st cluster st (12 cluster sts).

3rd Row. Sl st to center of ch 7, * ch 11, s c in center st of next loop and repeat from * all around.

4th Row. Sl st to center st of ch 11, 6 s c over same loop, 6 s c over next loop, * ch 11, 6 s c over next loop, 6 s c over next loop and repeat from * all around, ch 11, join to 1st s c of row.

5th Row. Ch 1, * 1 s c in each of the 1st 5 s c, skip 1 s c, 1 s c in each of the next 6 s c, ch 6, s c in center of ch 11 of previous row, ch 6 and repeat from *, join in 1st s c of row.

6th Row. * 1 s c in each s c omitting the 1st and last s c (9 s c), ch 6, s c in next loop, s c in s c, s c in next loop, ch 6 and repeat from * all around, join.

7th Row. Same as row 6 having 7 s c over the 9 s c of previous row and increasing 1 s c on each side of the 3 s c (5 s c).

8th Row. Same as row 7, work 5 s c over the 7 s c of previous row and increasing 1 s c on each side of the 5 s c (7 s c).

9th Row. Same as row 8, working 3 s c over the 5 s c of previous row and increasing 1 s c on each side of the 7 s c (9 s c).

10th Row. * 1 s c in center of 3 s c of previous row, ch 7, 1 s c over loop, 1 s c in each of the next 4 s c, ch 7, skip 1 s c, 1 s c in each of the next 4 s c, 1 s c in loop, ch 7 and repeat from * all around, break thread.

To join motifs in last row of 2nd motif, work as follows: 1 s c in center of 3 s c of previous row, ch 7, 1 s c in loop, 1 s c in each of the next 4 s c, ch 3, join to corresponding loop of 1st motif, ch 3, skip 1 s c, 1 s c in each of the next 4 s c of 2nd motif, 1 s c in loop, ch 3, join to next loop of 1st motif, ch 3, 1 s c in center of 3 s c of 2nd motif, ch 3, join to next loop of 1st motif, ch 3, s c in next loop of 2nd motif, 1 s c in each of the next 4 s c, ch 3, join to corresponding loop of 1st motif, ch 3, skip 1 s c, 1 s c in each of the next 4 s c of 2nd motif, 1 s c in loop and finish row same as 1st motif. Join all motifs in same manner.

Edge. Attach thread between 2 motifs, ch 5, skip 2 s c, d c in next s c, ch 5, sl st in top of d c just made for picot, ch 5, s c in next loop, ch 5, d c in s c at point, ch 5, sl st in top of d c for picot, ch 5, sl st in next loop, ch 5, skip 2 s c, d c in next s c, picot, ch 5, sl st in next loop and continue all around.

78

Sea Scallop

Continued from page 67

all around. 18th ROUND: Sl st to center of loop, * ch 5, sc in next loop, ch 3, sc in same loop, repeat from * 4 times, sc in next loop, ch 4, sl st in 1st st of ch for picot, sc in next loop, repeat from 1st * all around. 19th ROUND: Sl st to center of loop, sc in same loop, * ch 3, sc in same loop, ch 5, sc in next loop, repeat from * all around ending with ch 2, dc in 1st sc. 20th to 30th ROUND: Ch 3, sc in same space, ch 5, sc in next loop, repeat from beginning all around ending with ch 2, dc in dc. 31st ROUND: Ch 4, 2 trc in same space, * ch 2, 3 trc in next ch 5 loop, repeat from * all around, ch 2, join. 32nd ROUND: Sl st to next loop, ch 8, treble treble crochet (tr trc: 4 times over hook) in same space and * ch 2, tr trc in same space, repeat from * 4 times, * ch 5, skip 1 loop, sc in next loop, ch 5, skip 1 loop, 7 tr trc with ch 2 between each tr trc in next loop, repeat from * all around ending to correspond. 33rd ROUND: Ch 4, 2 dc in 1st st of ch, sc in next tr trc, repeat from beginning 5 times, 3 sc in each of the next 2 loops, sc in next tr trc, then repeat from beginning all around ending to correspond, join, cut thread.

Picot Picot

Continued from page 70

the next 2 sc, repeat from 1st * all around ending to correspond, join in 5th st of ch. 9th ROUND: Ch 1, sc in same space, work 1 sc in each d trc, 1 sc in each ch 2 loop and 3 sc in each ch 3 loop, join in 1st sc. 10th ROUND: Sl st over next 2 sc, ** work a double picot loop (double picot loop: * ch 7, sl st in 5th st from hook for picot, repeat from * once, ch 2), skip 4 sc, sc in next sc, repeat from ** twice, work a double picot loop, skip 1 sc, sc in next sc, * double picot loop, skip 4 sc, sc in next sc, repeat from * 6 times and continue all around ending to correspond, join. 11th ROUND: Sl st to center of next double picot loop, ch 3, dc in same space, * double picot loop, 2 dc in center of next double picot loop, repeat from * once, double picot loop, 2 trc, double picot loop, 2 trc in center of next double picot loop, * double picot loop, 2 dc in center of next double picot loop, repeat from * twice, work a single picot loop (single picot loop: ch 7, sl st in 5th st from hook for picot, ch 2), sc in center of next double picot loop, single picot loop, 2 dc in center of next double picot loop, repeat from 1st * all around ending to correspond, join. 12th ROUND: Sl st to center of double picot loop, ch 3, dc in same space, * double picot loop, 2 dc in center of next double picot loop, repeat from * once, double picot loop, 2 trc, double picot loop, 2 trc in center of next double picot loop, * double picot loop, 2 dc in center of next double picot loop, repeat from * twice, single picot loop, 2 dc before next single picot loop, 2 dc after next single picot loop, single picot loop, 2 dc in center of next double picot loop, repeat from 1st * all around ending to correspond, join. 13th ROUND: Sl st to center of next double picot loop, ch 3, 1 dc in same space, * double picot loop, 2 dc in center of next double picot loop, repeat from * once, double picot loop, 2 trc, double picot loop, 2 trc in center of next double picot loop, * double picot loop, 2 dc in center of next double picot loop, repeat from * twice, single picot loop, 2 dc after next single picot, 2 dc before next single picot, single picot loop, 2 dc in center of next double picot loop, repeat from 1st * all around ending to correspond, join in 3rd st of ch, cut thread.

Scroll Doily

Continued from page 72

ch 6, cluster st in next loop, picot, * ch 3, cluster st in same loop, picot, repeat from *, ch 3, d c in 1st s c.

7th Row. S c in same space, ch 3, s c in same space, * ch 6, s c in next loop, ch 3, s c in same space, ch 6, s c between next 2 cluster sts, ch 6, s c between next 2 cluster sts, ch 6, s c in next loop, ch 3, s c in same space, repeat from * all around ending row with ch 3, d c in 1st s c.

8th, 9th, 10th & 11th Rows. Same as 3rd row.

12th Row. S c in same space, ** ch 3, s c in same space, * ch 6, s c in next 6 ch loop, ch 3, s c in same space, repeat from *, ch 5, cluster st in next ch 6 loop, picot, ch 3, cluster st in same space, picot, ch 3, cluster st in same space, picot, (cluster st group), ch 5, s c in next ch 6 loop, repeat from ** all around in same manner.

13th Row. Sl st to center of next 6 ch loop, ch 3, s c in same space, * ch 6, s c in next loop, ch 3, s c in same space, ch 7, skip 1 loop, s c between next 2 cluster sts, ch 7, s c between next 2 cluster sts, ch 7, skip 1 loop, s c in next 6 ch loop, ch 3, s c in same space, repeat from * all around in same manner ending row with ch 3, d c in 1st s c.

14th Row. S c in same space, ch 3, s c in same space, ** ch 6, s c in next 6 ch loop, ch 3, s c in same space, * ch 6, s c in next 7 ch loop, ch 3, s c in same space, repeat from * twice, repeat from ** all around in same manner, ending row same as last row.

15th, 16th & 17th Rows. Same as 3rd row.

18th Row. Same as 12th row.

19th Row. Sl st to next 6 ch loop, ch 3, s c in same space, ch 6, s c in next loop, ch 3, s c in same space, * ch 6, skip 1 loop, cluster st group between next 2 cluster sts, cluster st group between next 2 cluster sts, ch 6, skip 1 loop, s c, ch 3, s c in next loop, ch 6, s c, ch 3, s c in next loop, repeat from * all around in same manner.

20th Row. Sl st to next 6 ch loop, ch 3, s c in same space, * ch 6, cluster st between 1st 2 cluster sts, picot, ch 3, cluster st in same space, picot, ch 3, cluster st between next 2 cluster sts, picot, ch 3, cluster st in same space, picot, ch 1, skip 2 center cluster sts, cluster st in next 3 ch loop, picot, ch 3, cluster st in same space, picot, ch 3, cluster st in next loop, picot, ch 3, cluster st in same space, picot, ch 6, skip 1 loop, s c, ch 3, s c in next loop, repeat from * all around, break thread.

Sea Spray

Continued from page 71

of next loop, ch 15, * in center st of next ch-9 make tr, ch 1, p, ch 1 and tr, ch 11. Repeat from * around. Join. **6th rnd:** Sl st to center of next loop, ch 17, * in center st of next ch-11 make tr, ch 1, p, ch 1 and tr, ch 13. Repeat from * around. Join.

7th rnd: Sl st to center of next loop, ch 1, sc in same loop, * ch 15, sc in center st of next loop. Repeat from * around, ending with sl st in 1st sc made. **8th rnd:** Ch 1, 9 sc in loop, * ch 8, tr tr in 8th ch from hook, ch 5, sc in tr tr, ch 7, sc in same place where tr tr was made, 9 sc in same loop, 9 sc in next loop. Repeat from * around. Sl st in 1st sc made. **9th rnd:** Sl st in next 3 sc, ch 9, * in ch-5 ring make (a 3-d tr cluster, ch 5) 5 times; skip 5 sc on 2nd half of loop, holding back the last loop of each tr on hook make tr in next sc, skip 3 sc of next loop, tr in next sc, thread over and draw through all loops on hook, ch 5. Repeat from * around. Join last tr with sl st in 4th st of ch-9. **10th rnd:** Ch 6, * skip next cluster, sc in center st of next loop, ch 5, in tip of next cluster make a 3-d tr cluster, ch 5 and 3-d tr cluster; in tip of next cluster make three 3-d tr clusters with ch-5 between, in tip of next cluster make 3-d tr cluster, ch 5 and 3-d tr cluster; ch 5, sc in center st of next loop, ch 3, dc in tip of the joined tr, ch 3. Repeat from * around. Join last ch-3 with sl st to 3rd st of ch-6. **11th rnd:** Sl st in next 3 ch, the sc and in the following 2 ch, 3 sc in same loop, * in each of next 4 loops make 5 sc, ch 3 and 5 sc; 3 sc in next loop, skip next 2 ch-3 sps, 3 sc in next loop. Repeat from * around. Join with sl st to 1st sc made. Fasten off.

Large Doily . . . Starting at center, ch 61 (to measure about 4¾ inches). **1st rnd:** 3 sc in 2nd ch from hook, sc in each ch across, 5 sc in last ch. Now, working along opposite side of foundation chain, make sc in each st across, ending with 2 sc in same place where first 3 sc were made. Join with sl st in 1st sc. **2nd rnd.** Ch 4, 2 tr in same place as sl st, 2 tr in each of next 3 sc, (ch 2, skip 2 sc, tr in next sc) 18 times; ch 2, skip next 2 sc, 2 tr in each of next 3 sc, 3 tr in next sc, 2 tr in each of next 3 sc, (ch 2, skip 2 sc, tr in next sc) 18 times; ch 2, skip next 2 sc, 2 tr in each of last 3 sc. Join with sl st in top st of ch-4. **3rd rnd:** Ch 4, holding back the last loop of each tr on hook make tr in next 2 sts, complete a 3-tr cluster, (ch 9, holding back the last loop of each tr on hook make tr in same place as last tr, tr in each of next 2 sts, complete a 3-tr cluster) 3 times; ch 9, cluster in next sp, ch 9, (cluster in next sp, ch 5, skip 1 sp, sc in next sp, ch 5, skip next sp, cluster in next sp, ch 9, skip 1 sp) twice; cluster in next sp, ch 5, skip 1 sp, sc in next sp, ch 5, skip 1 sp, cluster in next sp, ch 9, cluster in next space, ch 9, make a 3-tr cluster over 3 tr, make 6 more clusters with ch-9 between, having 1st tr of each cluster in same place as last tr of previous cluster, ch 9, cluster in next sp and work to correspond with other side, joining last ch-9 with sl st in tip of 1st cluster made. **4th to 8th rnds incl:** Work exactly as for Small Doily. **9th rnd:** Sl st in next 3 sc, ch 9, * in ch-5 ring make five 3-tr clusters with ch 5 between, ch 5, skip 5 sc on 2nd half of loop, holding back the last loop of each tr on hook make tr in next sc, skip 3 sc of next loop, tr in next sc, thread over and draw through all loops on hook, ch 5. Repeat from * 2 more times. Hold the next two ch-5 rings together and work the five 3-tr clusters over both of them. Continue thus around, working over two ch-5 rings on opposite side of doily. Join last ch-9 with sl st in 4th st of ch-9. **10th and 11th rnds:** Work exactly as for Small Doily. Fasten off.

Starch lightly and block to measurements given.

Floral Garland Doily

Continued from page 73

next loop, ch 7, sc in next loop, ch 7, skip 1 loop, sc in next loop. Repeat from * around, ending with ch 7. Join and break off.

Now complete scallops individually as follows: **1st row:** Skip first ch-3 loop, attach thread to next loop, (ch 3, sc in next loop) 18 times; dc in next loop, turn. **2nd row:** Sc in next loop, (ch 3, sc in next loop) 15 times; dc in next loop, turn. **3rd row:** Sc in next loop, (ch 3, sc in next loop) 12 times; dc in next loop, turn. **4th row:** Sc in next loop, (ch 3, sc in next loop) 10 times. Break off. Work each scallop in this manner.

EDGING . . . Attach thread to first ch-7 loop between any two scallops, ch 5, holding back on hook the last loop of each d tr make d tr in same loop, (d tr in next loop) twice; thread over and draw through all loops on hook (cluster made); (ch 4, sc in tip of cluster) 3 times (triple picot made); ch 5, sc in same loop as last d tr of cluster was made, * ch 5, holding back on hook the last loop of each d tr make d tr in same loop as last sc was made, (d tr in next free ch-3 loop) twice and complete cluster as before, ch 4, sc in tip of cluster (picot made), ch 5, sc in same loop as last d tr of cluster was made. Repeat from * once more; ** ch 5, holding back on hook the last loop of each d tr make d tr in same loop as last sc was made, skip next loop, d tr in next sc, skip next loop, d tr in next loop, and complete cluster as before, picot, ch 5, sc in same loop as last d tr of cluster was made. Repeat from ** 3 more times; make 2 more picot clusters to correspond with 2nd and 3rd picot clusters made, making last d tr of last picot cluster in next ch-7 loop, ch 5, make a cluster and triple picot as before, and continue thus around. Join and break off.

Victoriana

Continued from page 76

first shell made, ch 1, dc in same sp as last dc was made. Break off.

CENTER . . . 1st rnd: Attach Robinette to first joined loop of any scallop, ch 10, * holding back on hook the last loop of each tr, make 3 tr in the free loop of same scallop, thread over and draw through all loops on hook (cluster made), ch 5, holding back on hook the last loop of each d tr, make d tr in next joined-loop of same scallop and in first joined loop of next scallop, thread over and draw through all loops on hook (joint d tr made), ch 5. Repeat from * around, ending with d tr in last joined loop. Join with sl st to 5th ch of ch-10. **2nd rnd:** Ch 7, d tr in same place as sl st, * ch 2, cluster in tip of next cluster, ch 2, in tip of next joint d tr make d tr, ch 2 and d tr. Repeat from * around. Join to 5th ch of ch-7. **3rd rnd:** Ch 4, dc in next d tr, * ch 1, dc in tip of next cluster, (ch 1, dc in next d tr) twice. Repeat from * around. Join to 3rd ch of ch-4. Break off.

EDGING . . . 1st rnd: Attach Robinette to free loop of any small scallop, sc in same loop, * ch 5, cluster in first free loop on next scallop, ch 5, cluster in next loop, ch 5, in next loop make (cluster, ch 5) 5 times; (cluster in next loop, ch 5) twice; sc in free loop on next small scallop. Repeat from * around. Join. **2nd rnd:** * Sc in next sp, (ch 7, sc in next sp) 9 times. Repeat from * around. Join. **3rd rnd:** Sl st in first 2 ch of next loop, sc in same loop, * (ch 9, sc in next loop) 8 times; sc in next loop. Repeat from * around. Join. **4th rnd:** Sl st in first 3 ch of next loop, sc in same loop, * (ch 9, cluster in next loop) 7 times; sc in next loop. Repeat from * around. Join and break off. **5th rnd:** Attach Shaded Lt. Yellows to any loop, in each loop around make (3 sc, ch 3) 3 times and 3 sc. Join and break off.

Place doily on linen. Cut out material in back of doily, leaving ⅛ inch for hem. Sew hem neatly in place. Sew linen to doily. Starch lightly and press.

Edgings

Edgings That are Different

No. 8022 Starting at center of 1 fan, ch 8, join with sl st. **1st row:** 13 s c in ring. Ch 13, turn. **2nd row:** ** Make a Clones knot — *to make a Clones knot,* * *thread over, pass hook under ch, thread over and draw loop forward. Repeat from* * *7 more times, thread over and draw through all loops on hook, ch 1 to fasten,* s c in 4th ch from hook. Ch 3, skip 1 s c, tr tr in next s c, ch 7. Repeat from ** across. Ch 16, turn. **3rd row:** * A Clones knot, ch 4, tr tr in next tr tr, ch 8. Repeat from * across, ending with Clones knot, ch 4, tr tr in 6th st of turning ch. Ch 20, turn. **4th row:** * Tr tr in next tr tr, ch 14. Repeat from * across, ending with tr tr in 6th st of turning ch. Ch 4, turn. **5th row:** * Skip 1 st, d c in next st, ch 1. Repeat from * across. Fasten off. Make

another fan; do not break off, but ch 2, join with sl st to 3rd st of turning ch on last row of previous fan. Make necessary number of fans, joining in same way.

EDGING...Attach thread to 1st sp of 1st fan, * ch 5, s c in next sp. Repeat from * to within last sp of 1st fan, ch 2, skip 1 sp of 2nd fan, s c in next sp, ch 5 and continue thus across. Do not break off but work along straight edge as follows: **1st row:** 3 s c in 1st sp, * 11 s c in each of next 3 sps, 7 s c in next sp, 11 s c in each of next 3 sps, 3 s c in each of next 3 sps. Repeat from * across. Ch 5, turn. **2nd row:** * Skip 2 s c, d c in next s c, ch 2. Repeat from * across. Ch 5, turn. **3rd row:** * D c in next d c, ch 2. Repeat from * across. Fasten off.

No. 8357 EDGING No. 8357-A... **1st row:** Ch 10, d c in 10th ch from hook. Ch 10, turn. **2nd row:** D c in d c of previous row. Ch 10, turn. Repeat 2nd row until 12 loops are made. Ch 5, s c in next loop and in each of next 5 loops. Ch 2, turn and make s c in 1st s c made. Ch 5, d c in next d c. * Ch 10, turn and continue as before until 10 loops are made. Ch 5, s c in each of next 6 loops. Ch 2, turn and make s c in 1st s c, ch 5, d c in next d c. Repeat from * for desired length. Fasten off. Attach thread to 3rd last loop, s c in same loop, * ch 5, s c in next loop, ch 5, tr in each of next 2 loops, ch 5, s c in next loop. Repeat from * across. Fasten off.

INSERTION No. 8357-B...Work exactly as for No. 8357-A, but make a chain on both sides instead of one side.

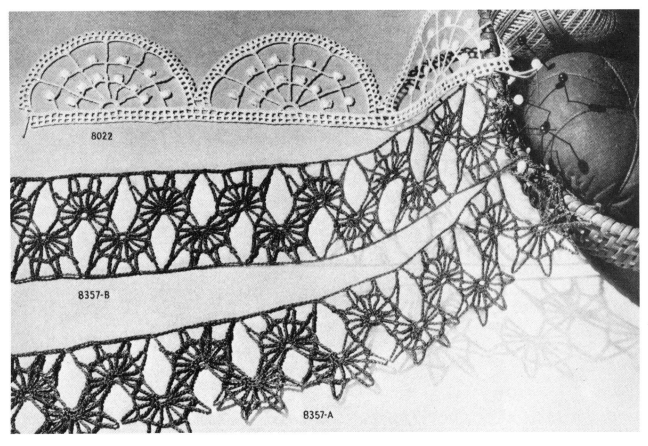

Rose Filet Edge

(Measure about 6 inches at the widest point)

Materials Required—
AMERICAN THREAD COMPANY
"STAR" MERCERIZED CROCHET COTTON, Article 30

1-125 yd. Ball White, size 50 will make about 7 inches of edge.
Steel Crochet Hook #13.

Ch 113, d c in 8th st from hook, 1 d c in each of the next **6 sts of ch,** * ch 2, skip 2 sts of ch, d c in next st, repeat from * 16 times, 1 d c in each of the next 3 sts of ch, * ch 2, skip 2 sts of ch, d c in next st, repeat from *, 1 d c in each of the next 6 sts of ch, ch 2, skip 2 sts of ch, 1 d c in each of the next 4 sts, * ch 2, skip 2 sts of ch, d c in next st, repeat from * 6 times, 1 d c in each of the next 3 sts of ch, ch 2, skip 2 sts of ch, d c in next st, ch 5, turn.

2nd Row—D c in d c, 1 d c in each of the next 3 d c, (solid mesh) * ch 2, d c in next d c, (open mesh), repeat from * 3 times, then work 3 solid meshes, 1 open mesh, 2 solid meshes, 4 open meshes, 1 solid mesh, 16 open meshes, 2 solid meshes, 1 open mesh, ch 5, turn.

3rd Row—D c in 1st d c, (an increase) 1 open mesh, 2 solid meshes, 13 open meshes, 3 solid meshes, 8 open meshes, 1 solid mesh, 2 open meshes, 1 solid mesh, 3 open meshes, 1 solid mesh, 1 open mesh, ch 5, turn.

Continue working up and down according to diagram to arrow. Repeat from beginning to arrow for desired length, break thread.
Attach thread in 1st mesh of lower edge at right hand corner, 2 s c in same mesh, ** 2 s c in next mesh, 5 s c

in next mesh, * 5 s c in next mesh, 2 s c in next mesh, repeat from *, 3 s c in next mesh, ch 4, sl st in last s c for picot, 2 s c in same mesh, * 2 s c in each of the next 2 meshes, picot, repeat from *, 2 s c in each of the next 3 meshes, picot, 2 s c in each of the next 2 meshes, picot, 2 s c in each of the next 2 meshes, 2 s c, picot, 3 s c in next mesh, * 2 s c in next mesh, 5 s c in next mesh, repeat from * 5 s c in next mesh, 2 s c in next mesh, picot, repeat from ** across lower edge. Work a row of s c across top edge alternating 2 s c in one open mesh and 3 s c in next mesh.

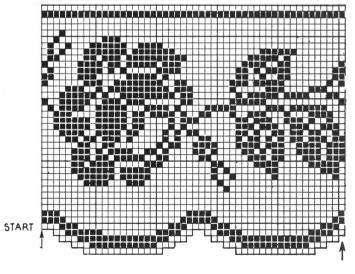

START

Dress Up Your Bed Linens

WE SUGGEST ROYAL PERLÉ

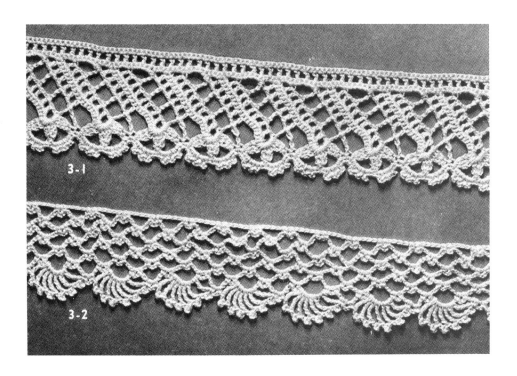

No. 3-1 . . . Starting at narrow end, ch 19. **1st row:** Tr in 11th ch from hook, (ch 3, sk 3 ch, tr in next ch) twice; ch 3, d tr in same place as last tr. Ch 5, turn. **2nd row:** Dc in d tr, (ch 1, sk 1 ch, dc in next ch, ch 1, dc in next tr) 3 times; (ch 1, sk 1 ch, dc in next ch) twice. Ch 1, turn. **3rd row:** (Sc in dc, sc in sp) 9 times; sc in 4th st of turning ch. Ch 5, turn. **4th row:** Dc in 1st sc, (ch 1, sk 1 sc, dc in next sc) 5 times. Ch 7, turn. **5th row:** (Sk next dc, tr in next dc, ch 3) twice; sk next dc, tr in 4th st of turning ch, ch 3, d tr in same place as last tr. Ch 5, turn. Repeat 2nd to 5th rows inclusive for length desired, ending with the 4th row. Fasten off.

SCALLOPS . . . **1st row:** Attach thread in center ch of 1st tr corner. Ch 4, * holding back the last loop of each tr on hook make 3 tr in next dc corner, thread over and draw through all loops on hook (3-tr cluster made), (ch 5, cluster in same corner) twice; tr in next dc corner. Repeat from * across. Ch 1, turn. **2nd row:** * Sc in tr, in next ch-5 loop make 2 sc, (ch 3, 1 sc) twice; ch 3 and 2 sc. Repeat from * across. Fasten off.

HEADING . . . **1st row:** Attach thread to 1st sp, ch 1, sc where thread was attached, * 2 sc in next sp, sc in next sc, sc in next ch, 2 sc in next sp, sc in top of next d tr, 4 sc in next sp, sc in next ch. Repeat from * across. Ch 4, turn. **2nd row:** * Sk next sc, dc in next sc, ch 1. Repeat from * across. Ch 1, turn. **3rd row:** Sc in each sp and each dc across. Fasten off.

No. 3-2 . . Make a chain slightly longer than desired length. **1st row:** Sc in 2nd ch from hook, ch 3, sc in next ch, * ch 7, sk 4 ch, sc in next ch, ch 3, sc in next ch. Repeat from * until 1st row is desired length, having an uneven number of ch-7 loops. Cut off remaining chain. Ch 10, turn. **2nd row:** * In next loop make sc, ch 3 and sc, ch 7. Repeat from * across, ending with ch 5, d tr in last sc. Ch 1, turn. **3rd row:** In 1st loop make sc, ch 3 and sc, * ch 7, in next loop make sc, ch 3 and sc. Repeat from * across. Ch 10, turn. **4th, 5th and 6th rows:** Repeat 2nd, 3rd and 2nd rows. Ch 8, turn. **7th row:** Sc in 3rd ch from hook (p made), in 1st loop make (d tr, ch 3, sc in 3rd ch from hook) 5 times and d tr; * in next loop make sc, ch 3 and sc, in next loop make (d tr, p) 6 times and d tr. Repeat from * across. Fasten off.

Wide Edgings
for Smartness

No. 8782 . . . Starting at narrow end of heading ch 8. **1st row:** In 8th ch from hook make 3 dc, ch 2 and 3 dc. Ch 5, turn. **2nd row:** In ch-2 sp (between dc groups) make 3 dc, ch 2 and 3 dc. Ch 5, turn. Repeat 2nd row for desired length being sure there is a multiple of seven ch-5 sps along both edges. Fasten off. **Next row:** Attach thread in 1st ch-5 sp, ch 1, sc in same place where thread was attached, * ch 5, sc in next ch-5 sp. Repeat from * across. Ch 4, turn. **Following row:** * (Skip 1 ch, dc in next ch, ch 1) twice; dc in next sc, ch 1. Repeat from * across. Fasten off. Attach thread in 1st ch-5 sp on opposite side and work to correspond but do not fasten off. Continue for scallop as follows: Ch 1, turn. **1st row:** Sc in 1st dc, (ch 6, skip 2 dc, sc in next dc) 5 times; ch 3, skip 2 dc, dc in last dc. Ch 1, turn. **2nd row:** In 1st and last loops make 4 sc, in each loop between make 7 sc. Ch 6, turn. **3rd row:** * Sc in center sc of loop below, ch 6. Repeat from * across ending with ch 3, dc in last sc of last loop. Ch 1, turn. **4th to 10th rows:** Repeat 2nd and 3rd rows alternately 3 times, then the 2nd row once more. At the end of the 10th row ch 3, turn. **11th row:** Dc in last sc of last loop. Fasten off.

NEXT SCALLOP—Attach thread in next dc of heading and work as for 1st scallop. Continue thus across. Fasten off.

EDGING—With right side facing, attach thread in 1st loop of 1st scallop; working along outside edge of scallops make 2 sc, ch 3 and 2 sc in the unfinished half of each outer loop, 2 sc in space between scallops. Continue thus across. Fasten off.

No. 8780 . . . Starting at narrow end, ch 43. **1st row:** Sc in 9th ch from hook, * ch 5, skip 3 ch, sc in next 5 ch, ch 5, skip 3 ch, sc in next ch. Repeat from * once more, ch 5, skip 3 ch, sc in next 6 ch. Ch 8, turn. **2nd row:** Dc at base of ch-8, * ch 5, skip 1 sc, sc in next 2 sc, (ch 5, sc in next loop) twice. Repeat from * across. Ch 3, turn. **3rd row:** 8 dc in loop, * sc in next loop, ch 5, sc in next loop, 9 dc in next loop. Repeat from * across. Ch 7, turn. **4th row:** Skip 2 dc, sc in next 5 dc, * ch 5, sc in next loop, ch 5, skip 2 dc, sc in next 5 dc. Repeat from * across. Ch 5, turn. **5th row:** * Skip 1 sc, sc in next 2 sc, (ch 5, sc in next loop) twice; ch 5. Repeat from * 2 more times, skip 1 sc, sc in next 2 sc, sc in next loop, ch 5, tr in same loop. Ch 5, turn. **6th row:** 9 dc in loop, * sc in next loop, ch 5, sc in next loop, 9 dc in next loop. Repeat from * across ending with sc in next loop, ch 5, sc in next loop. Ch 7, turn. **7th row:** Sc in loop, * ch 5, skip 2 dc, sc in next 5 dc, ch 5, sc in next loop. Repeat from * 2 more times; ch 5, skip 2 dc, sc in next 5 dc. Turn. **8th**

Continued on page 91

Enchanting Edgings

No. 8404 MOTIFS...Starting at center, ch 22. Join with sl st to form a ring. **1st rnd:** 44 s c in ring. **2nd rnd:** * Ch 5, s c in next s c, ch 5, s c in same s c, ch 5, s c in each of next 10 s c. Repeat from * around. **3rd rnd:** Sl st in each of next 3 ch of ch-5 loop, * ch 3, in next loop make s c, ch 5 and s c. Ch 3, s c in next loop, ch 3, s c in next loop. Repeat from * around. Fasten off. Make another motif same as this to within 3rd rnd.

3rd rnd: Sl st in each of next 3 ch of ch-5 loop, * ch 3, s c in next loop, ch 2, sl st in ch-5 loop of 1st motif, ch 2, s c back in same ch-5 of 2nd motif and complete as for 3rd rnd of previous motif. Fasten off. Make the necessary number of motifs for desired length, joining to previous motif as 2nd was joined to 1st, leaving 1 point free between joinings.

HEADING...**1st row:** Attach thread to free loop next to corner loop and in line with joining. Ch 10, d c in next loop, ch 2, s c in next center loop, * ch 2, d c in next loop, ch 4, tr tr in next ch-3 loop, tr tr in corresponding loop of next motif, ch 4, d c in next loop, ch 2, s c in next loop. Repeat from * across, ending row with tr tr in loop next to corner loop. Ch 1, turn. **2nd row:** 6 s c in 1st sp, s c in d c, 3 s c in next sp, s c in next s c, * 3 s c in next sp, s c in next d c, 6 s c in next sp, s c in each of next 2 tr tr, 6 s c in next sp, s c in next d c, 3 s c in next sp, s c in next s c. Repeat from * across. Ch 3, turn. **3rd row:** * Skip 3 s c, d c in next s c, ch 3, d c in same place as last d c. Repeat from * across, ending row with skip 3 s c, d c in last s c. Ch 1, turn. **4th row:** S c in d c, * 2 s c in sp, s c in each of 2 d c. Repeat from * across. Fasten off.

No. 8383 **1st row:** Ch 7, 4 d c in 7th ch from hook. Ch 7, turn. **2nd row:** 5 d c in last d c made. Ch 7, turn. Re-

peat the 2nd row for desired length. Ch 6, do not turn but work along long side as follows: **1st row:** * 4 d c in next ch-7 loop, ch 3, d c in d c at base of ch-7 loop, d c at base of same d c, ch 3. Repeat from * across, ending row with 4 d c in last loop. Ch 3, turn. **2nd row:** D c in each of 4 d c, d c in next ch, * ch 2, skip 2 ch of next ch-3, d c in next ch, d c in each of next 4 d c, d c in next ch. Repeat from * across. Ch 5, turn. **3rd row:** * Skip 2 sts, d c in next st, ch 2. Repeat from * across. Fasten off.

No. 8346 Make a chain slightly longer than desired length. **1st row:** D c in 8th ch from hook, * ch 2, skip 2 ch, d c in next ch. Repeat from * across. Ch 3, turn. **2nd row:** * 2 d c in ch-2 sp, d c in next d c, ch 4, skip 1 sp, s c in next sp, ch 4, skip 1 sp, d c in next d c. Repeat from * across, ending row with 4 d c. Ch 1, turn. **3rd row:** * S c in each of 4 d c, ch 9. Repeat from * across,

Continued on page 91

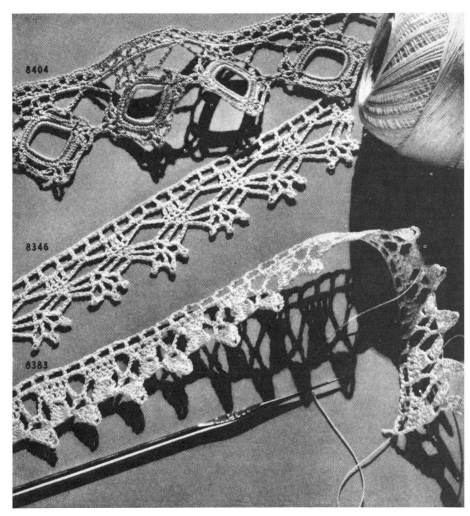

8404

8346

8383

Remember, Tatting Cotton for cobwebby fine touches—heavy Pearl Cotton for sturdy peasant effects.

Dainty Edgings for Handkerchiefs and Doilies

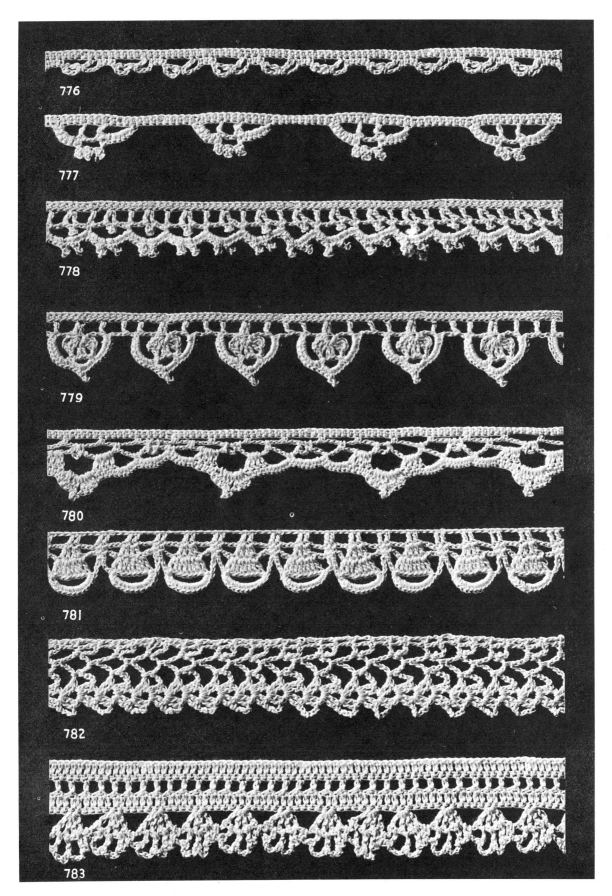

Dainty Edgings for Handkerchiefs and Doilies

ILLUSTRATED ON PAGES 88–89

For dainty Edging use American Thread Company "Silkine", Mercerized Crochet Cotton sizes 50 to 100 or "Silkine" Tatting Cotton, White or Colors.

No. 769

1st Row. Ch 10, thread over hook 5 times, insert in 10th st from hook work off loops two at a time leaving the last 2 on hook, tr c in same st, work off last 3 loops together, ch 15 and repeat from beginning for desired length.

2nd Row. 14 s c over 10 chain loop, 1 s c in each of the next 3 chs, picot, 1 s c in each of the next 2 chs and repeat for entire row.

No. 770

Make a ch the desired length and work one row of open meshes.

2nd Row. Ch 5, d c in mesh, * ch 5, sl st in 2nd st for picot, ch 1, d c in next mesh, ch 2, d c in next mesh, repeat from * across row.

No. 771

Ch 4, d c in 4th st from hook, * ch 3, turn, d c in d c, ch 6, sl st in base of 1st row, turn, 4 s c, p, 4 s c over loop, sl st in d c, ch 3, d c in d c, repeat from * for desired length and work a row of 6 ch loops on other side of edging.

No. 772

1st Row. Ch 9, turn, s c in third st from hook, 1 s c in each ch, ch 5, turn.

2nd, 4th and 6th Rows. d c in third s c, ch 2, skip 2 sts, d c in next st, ch 2 and turn.

3rd and 5th Rows. 2 s c in first mesh, s c in d c, 3 s c in next mesh, ch 5 and turn.

7th Row. 2 s c in first mesh, s c in d c, 3 s c in next mesh, ch 12, sl st in base of 4th row, ch 2, sl st in base of 2nd row and turn.

8th Row. 15 d c over ch, ch 6, turn, skip 4 d c, sl st in next st, ch 8, skip 4 d c, sl st in next st, ch 6, skip 4 d c, sl st in next st, ch 2, turn. 10 s c over first ch, 14 s c over next ch, 10 s c over last ch, d c in 1st s c of 7th row, * ch 2, skip 2 s c, d c in next s c repeat from * and repeat pattern for desired length.

No. 773

Work a row of s c.

2nd Row. * Ch 5, skip 3 sts, s c in next st, repeat from *.

3rd Row. 2 d c in loop, * ch 5, 2 d c in next loop, repeat from *.

4th Row. Ch 3, * 2 d c in loop, repeat from * twice, ch 2, 1 s c in next loop, repeat from beginning.

No. 774

Work 1 row of s c and 1 row of open meshes.

3rd Row. Ch 4, * 1 d c in next d c, ch 2, 1 d c in same d c, repeat from *.

4th Row. Ch 4, ** tr c in loop, * picot, tr c in same loop, repeat from * twice, ch 3, 1 s c in next loop, ch 5, picot, ch 1, s c in next loop, ch 3, repeat from **.

No. 775

Work a chain for desired length or a row of s c over material and work 1 row of open meshes.

3rd Row. ** work s c over 3 meshes. Ch 7, turn, sl st over 2nd d c, ch 1, turn, 15 s c over loop, s c over next open mesh, ch 2, turn, * skip 1 s c, 1 d c in next s c, ch 2, repeat from * 6 times, ch 2, sl st above next d c, ch 1, turn, * 2 s c in loop, picot, repeat from * 6 times, 2 s c over last loop, 8 s c over corner loop, repeat from **.

No. 776

Work a row of s c.

2nd Row. * 3 s c, ch 4, 1 d c in first s c, ch 4, 1 d c in top of last d c made, skip 4 s c and repeat from *.

No. 777

Work 12 s c over material, ** ch 4, turn, skip 3 sts, 1 d c in next st, ch 2, skip 2 sts, 1 d c in next st, ch 4, skip 3 sts, sl st in next st, turn, 5 s c over loop, 1 s c in d c, * ch 4, sl st in first st for picot, repeat from * twice, 1 s c in d c, 5 s c over loop, work 20 s c over material and repeat from **.

No. 778

Work a row of s c.

2nd Row. Ch 4, skip 2 sts, 1 d c in next st, ch 2, * skip 2 sts, 1 d c in next st, picot, 1 d c in same st, ch 2, skip 2 sts, 1 d c in next st, ch 2, repeat from *.

3rd Row. * Ch 5, 1 s c in single d c, repeat from *.

4th Row. * 3 s c over loop, picot, 2 s c over loop, picot, 3 s c over loop, repeat from *.

No. 779

Work a row of s c.

2nd Row. Ch 5, * skip 2 sts, 1 d c in next st, ch 2, skip 2 sts, 1 d c in next st, ch 2, skip 3 sts, 2 d c in next st, ch 5, 2 d c in last d c made, ch 2, 2 d c in same space, ch 2, 1 d c in same space, ch 2, sl st in same space, ch 2, skip 3 sts, 1 d c in next st, ch 5, turn work, 1 s c in 2 ch loop, ch 4, 1 s c in next loop, ch 5, sl st in next d c, ch 5, turn work, 8 s c over loop, 3 s c, picot 3 s c over next loop, 8 s c over next loop, ch 2 and repeat from *.

No. 780

Work a row of s c.

2nd Row. * Ch 6, skip 5 sts, 1 s c in next st, repeat from *.

3rd Row. S c in loop, * ch 6, 1 s c in next loop, ch 3, 1 s c in same loop, ch 6, 1 s c in next loop, repeat from *.

4th Row. * Ch 4, 4 d c in loop, ch 5, skip picot, 4 d c in next loop, ch 3, 1 s c in next loop, ch 4, 1 s c in next loop, repeat from *.

5th Row. * 6 s c in loop, 1 s c in each d c, 4 d c in next loop, picot, 4 d c in same loop, 1 s c in each d c, 6 s c in next loop, 8 s c over next loop, repeat from *.

No. 781

Ch for desired length or work a row of s c.

2nd Row. * Ch 3, skip 2 sts 1 d c in each of the next 2 sts, repeat from *.

3rd Row. * Ch 3, 2 d c in each of the next 2 d c, ch 3, 1 s c in each of the next 2 d c, repeat from *.

4th Row. * Ch 3, 2 d c in each d c, ch 8, turn, sl st in 1st d c, ch 1, turn, 12 s c over loop, ch 3, 1 s c in each s c, repeat from *.

No. 782

Ch 17, 2 d c in 8th st from hook, ch 2, 2 d c in same st, ch 4, skip 3 sts, 1 s c in next st, ch 4, skip 3 sts, 1 d c in each of the last 2 sts, ch 3, turn.

2nd Row. 1 d c in 2nd d c, ch 4, 1 s c in loop, ch 4, 1 s c in next loop, ch 4, 2 d c in center of shell, ch 2, 2 d c in same space, ch 5, turn.

3rd Row. 2 d c in shell, ch 2, 2 d c in same space, ch 4, 1 s c in center loop, ch 4, 1 d c in each d c, repeat the last 2 rows for desired length.

No. 783

Work a chain the desired length and work 1 row of d c, 1 row of 1 ch meshes and 1 row of d c.

4th Row. Ch 3, ** skip 5 sts, 1 d c in next st, * ch 1, 1 d c in same st, repeat from * twice, ch 3 and repeat from ** to end of row.

5th Row. * 1 s c in ch, ch 2, 1 d c in first ch of shell, ch 4, d c in next ch, ch 4, d c in next ch, ch 3, repeat from *.

Wide Edgings for Smartness

No. 8780 —*Continued from page 86*

row: Sl st in next st, ch 1, sc in same place, sc in next st, * (ch 5, sc in next loop) twice; ch 5, skip 1 sc, sc in next 2 sc. Repeat from * 2 more times; (ch 5, sc in next loop) twice. Ch 3, turn. **9th row:** 8 dc in loop, * sc in next loop, ch 5, sc in next loop, 9 dc in next loop. Repeat from * across ending with sc in last loop. Turn.

10th row: Sl st in next 2 sts, sc in next 5 sts, * ch 5, sc in next loop, ch 5, skip 2 dc, sc in next 5 dc. Repeat from * across. Ch 5, turn. **11th row:** Skip 1 sc, sc in next 2 sc, * (ch 5, sc in next loop) twice; ch 5, skip 1 sc, sc in next 2 sc. Repeat from * 2 more times. Ch 3, turn. **12th row:** Sc in next loop, * 9 dc in next loop, sc in next loop, ch 5, sc in next loop. Repeat from * across. Ch 7, turn. **13th row:** Sc in loop, * ch 5, skip 2 dc, sc in next 5 dc, ch 5, sc in next loop. Repeat from * once more, ch 5, skip 2 dc, sc in next 6 dc. Ch 8, turn. Repeat the 2nd to 13th rows incl. for length desired. Fasten off. Work along scalloped edge as follows: Attach thread to last sc at end of 1st row worked. **1st row:** (Ch 5, sc in next loop) 4 times; ch 5, skip 2 dc, sc in next st (point), then work 4 loops along other side of scallop to correspond. Continue in this manner to end of row. Turn. **2nd row:** 7 sc in each of 1st 4 loops, * 3 sc in next loop, ch 3, sc in 3rd ch from hook, 3 sc in same loop (point), 7 sc in each of next 8 loops. Repeat from * across. Fasten off.

ILLUSTRATED ON PAGE 86

No. 8340 . . . **1st row:** Ch 57. Dc in 4th ch from hook and in next 10 ch, ch 11, skip 5 ch, dc in next ch, (ch 2, skip 2 ch, dc in next ch) twice; ch 11, skip 5 ch, dc in next 18 ch, then ch 3, skip 2 ch, sc in next ch, ch 3, skip 2 ch,

dc in next ch (lacet made); dc in next 2 ch. Ch 3, turn. *Hereafter work only through back loops of stitches throughout, except when making ch-2 sps.* **2nd row:** Dc in next 2 dc, ch 5, dc in 17 dc, sl st in 3rd st of ch and in next 6 ch, * ch 2, skip 1 sp, dc in next dc, ch 2, skip 1 sp, sl st in 3rd st of next ch and in next 6 ch, skip 1 dc, dc in next 10 dc and in top of turning ch. * Ch 8, turn. **3rd row:** * Dc in 4th ch from hook and in next 4 ch, dc in 6 dc, ch 11, skip 5 dc, dc in next st, (ch 2, skip 2 sts, dc in next st) twice; * ch 24, skip 2 sps, dc in next sl st, (ch 2, skip 2 sts, dc in next st) twice; ch 11, skip 5 dc, dc in next 12 dc, make a lacet, then dc in next dc and in top of turning ch. Ch 3, turn. **4th row:** Dc in next 2 dc, ch 5, dc in 11 dc, sl st in 3rd st of ch and in next 6 ch, ch 2, skip 1 sp, dc in next dc, ch 2, skip 1 sp, sl st in 3rd st of next ch. Working into each st of ch make sc, h dc, dc, 2 tr, dc, h dc, sc, 2 sl sts, sc, h dc, dc, 2 tr, dc, h dc, sc and sl st (2 petals made). Repeat between *'s of 2nd row, ch 8, turn. **5th row:** Repeat between *'s of 3rd row, ch 24, skip 2 sps, 2 petals and 2 sps; dc in next sl st, (ch 2, skip 2 sts, dc in next st) twice; ch 11, skip 5 dc, dc in next 6 dc, make a lacet and finish as for 3rd row. Ch 3, turn. **6th row:** Dc in next 2 dc, ch 5, dc in 5 dc, sl st in 3rd st of ch and in next 6 ch, ch 2, skip 1 sp, dc in next dc, ch 2, sl st in 3rd st of next ch. Make 2 petals as before, then repeat between *'s of 2nd row. Ch 8, turn. **7th row:** Repeat between *'s of 3rd row, ch 36, skip 2 sps, 2 petals and 2 sps; dc in next sl st, (ch 2, skip 2 sts, dc in next st) twice; ch 10, skip 4 dc, dc in next dc, and finish row as before. Ch 3, turn. **8th row:** Dc in next 2 dc, ch 5, skip lacet, sl st in 3rd st of next ch and in next 5 ch, ch 2, skip 1 sp, dc in next dc, ch 2, skip 1 sp, sl st in 3rd st of next ch and in next 6 ch. Make 2 petals, then sl st in next 6 ch. Repeat between *'s of 2nd row,

ch 1, turn. **9th row:** * Skip 1st dc, sl st in next 6 dc (6 dc decreased); ch 3, dc in next 4 dc and in 7 sl sts, ch 11, skip 2 sps, dc in next sl st, (ch 2, skip 2 sts, dc in next st) twice *; ch 37, skip 2 petals, dc in next sl st, (ch 2, skip 2 sts, dc in next st) twice; ch 11, skip 2 sps, dc in 6 sl sts, and finish row as before. Ch 3, turn. **10th row:** Dc in next 2 dc, ch 5, dc in 5 dc, sl st in 3rd st of ch and in next 6 ch, ch 2, skip 1 sp, dc in next dc, ch 2, skip 1 sp, sl st in 3rd st of next ch and in next 6 ch. Then working into each ch make sc, h dc, dc, 2 tr, dc, h dc, sc and sl st, then make sc under all petals at center, skip 1 ch, then continue along ch as before, making sl st, sc, h dc, dc, 2 tr, dc, h dc, sc and 7 sl sts. Repeat between *'s of 2nd row, ch 1, turn. **11th row:** Repeat between *'s of 9th row, ch 11, skip 2 petals, dc in next sl st, (ch 2, skip 2 sts, dc in next st) twice; ch 11, skip 2 sps, dc in 7 sl sts and in 5 dc, and finish row. Ch 3, turn. **12th row:** Dc in next 2 dc, ch 5, dc in 11 dc, sl st in 3rd st of ch and in next 6 ch, ch 2, skip 1 sp, dc in next dc, ch 2, skip 1 sp, sl st in 3rd st of next ch and in next 6 ch. Repeat between *'s of 2nd row, ch 1, turn. **13th row:** Repeat between *'s of 9th row, ch 11, skip 2 sps, dc in 7 sl sts and 11 dc, and finish row. Ch 3, turn. **14th row:** Same as 2nd row. Repeat 3rd to 14th rows incl. for length desired. Fasten off.

EDGING: Attach thread to last dc at scalloped edge of last row, * ch 3, dc in corner between 2 points, ch 4, sl st in top of dc (p made), work 2 more p's, ch 3, sc in last dc of next point. Repeat from * 2 more times, ch 3, dc between next 2 rows, 3 p's, ch 3, sc at next point. Make 2 more "p" groups across other half of scallop to correspond with first half, ch 3, dc between next 2 rows (between scallops), 3 p's, ch 3, sc in next point, and continue thus across. Fasten off.

Enchanting Edgings

No. 8346...*Continued from page 87*

ending row with 4 s c. Ch 1, turn. **4th row:** S c in each of 3 s c, * ch 4, skip 4 ch of ch-9, in next ch make d c, ch 2

and d c. Ch 4, skip 1 s c, s c in each of next 3 s c. Repeat from * across. Ch 1, turn. **5th row:** Skip 1 s c, s c in next s c, ** ch 4, in ch-2 sp make: d c, * ch

5, sl st in 4th ch from hook (1 p made), ch 1, d c in same ch-2. Repeat from * 2 more times, ch 4, skip 1 s c, s c in next s c. Repeat from ** across.

Simplicity in Easily Worked Edgings

WE SUGGEST ROYAL SOCIETY CORDICHET, SIZE 20
OR ROYAL PERLÉ, SIZE 5

No. 3-17 . . . Starting at one narrow end, ch 38. **1st row:** Dc in 8th ch from hook, (ch 2, sk 2 ch, dc in next ch) 10 times. Ch 5, turn. **2nd row:** Dc in next dc, (ch 2, dc in next dc) 9 times; ch 2, sk 2 ch, dc in next ch (11 sps made); then ch 8, sk 2 ch, sc in next ch (at base of 1st row). Turn. **3rd row:** 5 sc in ch-8 loop, ch 5, sl st in 5th ch from hook (p made), 5 sc in same loop, sc in dc, * in next sp work dc and tr, in next dc work 2 d tr with ch 1 between, in next sp work tr and dc, then sc in next dc. Repeat from * 3 more times; ch 3, dc in next dc, ch 2, dc in next dc, ch 2, sk 2 ch, dc in next ch. Ch 5, turn. **4th row:** Dc in next dc, ch 2, dc in next dc, ch 2, sk 2 ch, dc in next ch, ch 2, sc in ch-1 sp, (ch 5, sc in next ch-1 sp) 3 times; ch 2, tr in next sc. Ch 5, turn. **5th row:** Dc in next sc, (ch 2, sk 2 ch, dc in next ch, ch 2, dc in next sc) 3 times; (ch 2, dc in next dc) 3 times; ch 2, sk 2 ch, dc in next ch. Ch 5, turn. **6th row:** Dc in next dc, (ch 2, dc in next dc) 9 times; ch 2, sk 2 ch, dc in next ch, ch 8, sc in tr at end of 4th row. Turn. Repeat the 3rd to 6th rows inclusive for length desired, ending with the 5 sc, p and 5 sc at beginning of 3rd row.

No. 3-18 . . . Starting at bottom of chart, ch 26. **1st row:** Dc in 8th ch from hook, (ch 2, sk 2 ch, dc in next ch) 3 times; dc in next 3 ch, (ch 2, sk 2 ch, dc in next ch) twice. Ch 5, turn. **2nd row:** Dc in next dc, 2 dc in sp, dc in next dc (bl over sp made), dc in next 3 dc (bl over bl made), (ch 2, dc in next dc) 3 times (3 sps over 3 sps made). Ch 7, turn. **3rd row:** Dc in 1st dc (1 sp increased), 3 sps, 1 bl, ch 2, sk 2 dc, dc in next dc (sp over bl made), make 1 more sp. Ch 5, turn. Starting with 4th row, follow chart to top. Repeat entire chart for length desired. Work a row of sc evenly along both straight and scalloped edges. Fasten off.

CHART
No. 3-18

No. 3-19 . . . Make a chain slightly longer than length desired. **1st row:** Sc in 2nd ch from hook and in next 3 ch, * ch 5, sk 4 ch, dc in next 5 ch, ch 5, sk 4 ch, sc in next 7 ch. Repeat from * across for length desired, ending with 4 sc. Ch 1, turn. Cut off remaining chain. **2nd row:** Sc in 3 sc, * ch 5, sk 4 ch, dc in next ch, dc in next 2 dc, ch 3, sk 1 dc, dc in next 2 dc and in next ch, ch 5, sk 1 sc, sc in next 5 sc. Repeat from * across, ending with 3 sc. Ch 1, turn. **3rd row:** Sc in 2 sc, * ch 5, sk 3 ch, dc in next 2 ch, dc in next dc, ch 5, sc in next sp, ch 5, sk 2 dc, dc in next dc and in next 2 ch, ch 5, sk 1 sc, sc in 3 sc. Repeat from * across, ending with 2 sc. Ch 1, turn. **4th row:** Sc in sc, * ch 5, sk 3 ch, dc in next 2 ch, dc in next dc, ch 5, sc in loop, ch 7, sc in next loop, ch 5, sk 2 dc, dc in next dc and in next 2 ch, ch 5, sk 1 sc, sc in next sc. Repeat from * across, ending with sc. Turn. **5th row:** Sl st in next 4 ch, ch 3, dc in next ch and in next dc, ch 5, then holding back on hook the last loop of each tr, work 3 tr in ch-7 loop, thread over and draw through all loops on hook (cluster made); work * (ch 5, dc in 5th ch from hook, cluster in same loop) 4 times; ch 5, sk 2 dc, dc in next dc and in next 2 ch, sk next sc and next 3 ch, work dc in next 2 ch and in next dc, ch 5, cluster in next loop. Repeat from * across, ending with 3 dc. Fasten off.

Infinite Beauty in Small Design

WE SUGGEST ROYAL SOCIETY CORDICHET, SIZES 30-50

No. 3-22 . . . Starting at narrow end, ch 11. **1st row:** Dc in 4th ch from hook and in next 7 ch. Ch 10, turn. **2nd row:** Make a cross st as follows: Thread over twice, insert hook in next dc and draw loop through, thread over and draw through 2 loops on hook, thread over, sk 2 dc, insert hook in next dc and draw loop through, thread over and draw through 2 loops 4 times; ch 2, insert hook in center of cross and draw loop through, then complete as for a dc (cross st made). Ch 1, sk 1 dc, make another cross st (making 2nd leg in top of turning ch), ch 15, sc in same place as 2nd leg of cross st. Turn. **3rd row:** In ch-15 loop make sc, h dc and 20 dc, dc in next st, 2 dc in next sp, dc in next st, dc in next sp, dc in next st, 2 dc in next sp, dc in next st. Ch 10, turn. **4th row:** Dc in next dc, (ch 1, sk 1 dc, dc in next dc) 4 times. Ch 3, turn. **5th row:** (Dc in next sp, dc in next dc) 4 times. Ch 10, turn. Repeat the 2nd to 5th rows inclusive for length desired, ending with 3rd row. Do not fasten off but ch 9 to turn and work heading along top edge as follows: * Tr in next loop, ch 2, tr in same loop, ch 2. Repeat from * across, ending with ch 9, sl st at base of last dc of 1st row of edging. Fasten off.

No. 3-23 . . . Starting at narrow end, ch 9. **1st row:** Thread over twice, insert hook in 5th ch from hook and pull loop through; thread over and draw through 2 loops on hook, thread over, sk 2 ch, insert hook in next ch and pull loop through, (thread over and draw through 2 loops) 4 times; ch 2, dc in center point of cross (cross st made), tr in last ch. Ch 4, turn. **2nd row:** Tr in 1st leg of cross st, 2 tr in ch-2 sp, tr in last leg of cross st, tr in top st of turning ch. Ch 4, turn. **3rd row:** Thread over twice, insert hook in next tr and pull loop through; thread over and draw through 2 loops on hook, thread over, sk 2 tr, insert hook in next tr and pull loop through, complete cross st as before, tr in top st of turning ch. Ch 4, turn. Repeat 2nd and 3rd rows alternately for length desired, ending with a cross st. Ch 1 and work scallops along long edge as follows: **1st row:** Sc in top of last tr, * ch 6, sc in base of same tr, ch 6, sc in top of next tr. Repeat from * across. Ch 5, turn. **2nd row:** * Make 9 tr in next loop, dc in next loop. Repeat from * across, ending with 9 tr in last loop. Ch 5, turn. **3rd row:** Sk next tr, * tr in center 5 tr of this group, ch 5, sc in next dc, ch 5, sk 2 tr of next group. Repeat from * across, ending with tr in center 5 tr of last group. Ch 4, turn. **4th row:** * Holding back the last loop of each tr on hook make tr in next 3 tr, thread over and draw through all loops on hook (cluster made), in tip of cluster just made make ch 3, sc, ch 5, sc, ch 3 and sc, ch 5, holding back the last loop of each dc on hook make dc in each of next 2 loops, thread over and draw through all loops on hook, ch 5, sk 1 tr. Repeat from * across. Fasten off.

Edgings for the Bath

Washcloth . . . S-522

J. & P. COATS "KNIT-CRO-SHEEN," Art. A.64: 1 ball each of No. 1 White, No. 10-A Canary Yellow and No. 12 Black.

Milwards Steel Crochet Hook No. 7.

A washcloth.

Starting with Yellow, ch 2. **1st row:** Sc in 2nd ch from hook. Ch 5, turn. **2nd row:** In sc make dc, ch 1 and dc. Ch 1, turn. **3rd row:** Sc in ch-1 sp. Ch 5, turn. Repeat 2nd and 3rd rows alternately until piece reaches around washcloth, allowing for corners. Break off.

HEADING . . . Now working along straight side of edging, attach White to first st, sc in same place, * ch 3, skip dc row, sc in next sp. Repeat from * across. Break off.

SCALLOPED EDGE . . . Attach Black to opposite side, sc in sc, * ch 3, sc in ch-5 loop, ch 3, sc in next sc. Repeat from * across. Break off. Attach White to first Black sc, sc in same place, ch 3, * holding back on hook the last loop of each sc, insert hook in first ch-3 sp, thread over and draw loop through, insert hook in next ch-3 sp, thread over and draw loop through, thread over and draw through all loops on hook (joint sc), ch 3, sc in next sc, ch 3. Repeat from * across. Break off. Sew edging to washcloth.

Guest Towel . . S-523

COATS & CLARK'S O.N.T. TATTING-CRO-CHET, Art. C.21, Size 70: 2 balls of No. 1 White and 1 ball of No. 9 Yellow . . . a few yards of White "Knit-Cro-Sheen."

Milwards Steel Crochet Hook No. 14.

A grey guest towel.

Each motif measures 1¼ inches in diameter

RING MOTIF—First Ring . . . Starting at center with White, ch 8. Join with sl st to form ring. **1st rnd:** Working over 3 strands of "Knit-Cro-Sheen" make 16 sc in ring. Join with sl st to first sc. Break off.

SECOND RING . . . Work as for First Ring and join to First Ring by making a sl st in any sc. Make 3 more rings, joining the same way and leaving 3 sc free on inner edge and 11 sc free on outer edge. Join last ring to first ring.

Now work around rings as follows: **1st rnd:** Attach White to 4th free sc on any ring, sc in same place, * (ch 4, sl st in 3rd ch from hook—picot made) twice; ch 1, skip 3 sc, sc in next sc, (ch 1, picot) twice; ch 1, skip first 3 sc on next ring, sc in next sc. Repeat from * around. Join. **2nd rnd:** Sl st to center of next loop between picots, sc in same place, * (ch 1, picot) twice; ch 1, sc in center of next loop. Repeat from * around. Join and break off.

FLOWER MOTIF . . . Starting at center with Yellow, ch 10. Join with sl st to form ring. Working over 3 strands of "Knit-Cro-Sheen," make sc in ring, then make 9 sc over "Knit-Cro-Sheen" only, * ch 1, turn, still working over "Knit-Cro-Sheen," make sc in each of 9 sc just made, 2 sc in ring, turn; skip first 2 sc, sc in first 5 sc on petal, make 4 sc over "Knit-Cro-Sheen" only. Repeat from * until 10 petals have been completed, ending with 1 sc in ring. Join to first sc made. Break off. Sew last petal to first petal.

Now work around flower as follows: Attach White to tip of any petal, sc in same place, ch 1, picot, sl st in any loop on Ring Motif, picot, ch 1, sc in tip of next petal, ch 1, picot, sl st in next loop on Ring Motif, picot, ch 1, sc in tip of next petal, * (ch 1, picot) twice; ch 1, sc in tip of next petal. Repeat from * around. Join and break off.

Make another Ring Motif, join to Flower Motif as before leaving 3 loops free on each side of joining. Continue in this manner, alternating Flower and Ring Motifs until piece is long enough to reach across towel, ending with a Ring Motif.

HEADING . . . 1st row: Attach White to 3rd free loop preceding joining on First Motif, ch 9, dc in same loop, * ch 5, sc in next loop, ch 5, dc in next loop, ch 5, holding back on hook the last loop of each tr make tr in same loop and in first free loop on next motif, thread over and draw through all loops on hook (joint tr made), ch 5, dc in same loop. Repeat from * across, ending with dc, ch 5 and tr in 3rd free loop on last motif. Ch 8, turn. **2nd row:** * Skip next 5 ch, dc in next st. Repeat from * across. Break off.

Make another piece the same way. Sew to towel.

Simple Crochet Stitches

No. 1—Chain Stitch (CH) Form a loop on thread insert hook on loop and pull thread through tightening threads. Thread over hook and pull through last chain made. Continue chains for length desired.

No. 2—Slip Stitch (SL ST) Make a chain the desired length. Skip one chain, * insert hook in next chain, thread over hook and pull through stitch and loop on hook. Repeat from *. This stitch is used in joining and whenever an invisible stitch is required.

No. 3—Single Crochet (S C) Chain for desired length, skip 1 ch, * insert hook in next st, thread over hook and pull through ch. There are now 2 loops on hook, thread over hook and pull through both loops, repeat from *. For succeeding rows of s c, ch 1, turn insert hook in top of next st taking up both threads and continue same as first row.

No. 4—Short Double Crochet (S D C) Ch for desired length thread over hook, insert hook in 3rd st from hook, draw thread through (3 loops on hook), thread over and draw through all three loops on hook. For succeeding rows, ch 2, turn.

No. 5—Double Crochet (D C) Ch for desired length, thread over hook, insert hook in 4th st from hook, draw thread through (3 loops on hook) thread over hook and pull through 2 loops thread over hook and pull through 2 loops. Succeeding rows, ch 3, turn and work next d c in 2nd d c of previous row. The ch 3 counts as 1 d c.

No. 6—Treble Crochet (TR C) Ch for desired length, thread over hook twice insert hook in 5th ch from hook draw thread through (4 loops on hook) thread over hook pull through 2 loops thread over, pull through 2 loops, thread over, pull through 2 loops. For succeeding rows ch 4, turn and work next tr c in 2nd tr c of previous row. The ch 4 counts as 1 tr c.

No. 7—Double Treble Crochet (D TR C) Ch for desired length thread over hook 3 times insert in 6th ch from hook (5 loops on hook) and work off 2 loops at a time same as tr c. For succeeding rows ch 5 turn and work next d tr c in 2nd d tr c of previous row. The ch 5 counts as 1 d tr c.

No. 8—Rib Stitch. Work this same as single crochet but insert hook in back loop of stitch only. This is sometimes called the slipper stitch.

No. 9—Picot (P) There are two methods of working the picot. (A) Work a single crochet in the foundation, ch 3 or 4 sts depending on the length of picot desired, sl st in top of s c made. (B) Work an s c, ch 3 or 4 for picot and s c in same space. Work as many single crochets between picots as desired.

No. 10—Open or Filet Mesh (O M.) When worked on a chain work the first d c in 8th ch from hook * ch 2, skip 2 sts, 1 d c in next st, repeat from *. Succeeding rows ch 5 to turn, d c in d c, ch 2, d c in next d c, repeat from *.

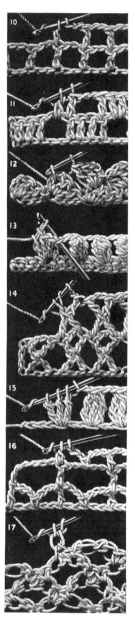

No. 11—Block or Solid Mesh (S M) Four double crochets form 1 solid mesh and 3 d c are required for each additional solid mesh. Open mesh and solid mesh are used in Filet Crochet.

No. 12—Slanting Shell St. Ch for desired length, work 2 d c in 4th st from hook, skip 3 sts, sl st in next st, * ch 3, 2 d c in same st with sl st, skip 3 sts, sl st in next st. Repeat from *. **2nd Row.** Ch 3, turn 2 d c in sl st, sl st in 3 ch loop of shell in previous row, * ch 3, 2 d c in same space, sl st in next shell, repeat from *.

No. 13—Bean or Pop Corn Stitch. Work 3 d c in same space, drop loop from hook insert hook in first d c made and draw loop through, ch 1 to tighten st.

No. 14—Cross Treble Crochet. Ch for desired length, thread over twice, insert in 5th st from hook, * work off two loops, thread over, skip 2 sts, insert in next st and work off all loops on needle 2 at a time, ch 2, d c in center to complete cross. Thread over twice, insert in next st and repeat from *.

No. 15—Cluster Stitch. Work 3 or 4 tr c in same st always retaining the last loop of each tr c on needle, thread over and pull through all loops on needle.

No. 16—Lacet St. Ch for desired length, work 1 s c in 10th st from hook, ch 3 skip 2 sts, 1 d c in next st, * ch 3, skip 2 sts, 1 s c in next st, ch 3, skip 2 sts 1 d c in next st, repeat from * to end of row, 2nd row, d c in d c, ch 5 d c in next d c.

No. 17—Knot Stitch (Sometimes Called Lovers Knot St.) Ch for desired length, * draw a ¼ inch loop on hook, thread over and pull through ch, s c in single loop of st, draw another ¼ inch loop, s c into loop, skip 4 sts, s c in next st, repeat from *. To turn make ⅜″ knots, * s c in loop at right of s c and s c in loop at left of s c of previous row, 2 knot sts and repeat from *.

Metric Conversion Chart

CONVERTING INCHES TO CENTIMETERS AND YARDS TO METERS

mm — millimeters   cm — centimeters   m — meters

INCHES INTO MILLIMETERS AND CENTIMETERS
(Slightly rounded off for convenience)

inches	mm		cm	inches	cm	inches	cm	inches	cm
⅛	3mm			5	12.5	21	53.5	38	96.5
¼	6mm			5½	14	22	56	39	99
⅜	10mm	or	1cm	6	15	23	58.5	40	101.5
½	13mm	or	1.3cm	7	18	24	61	41	104
⅝	15mm	or	1.5cm	8	20.5	25	63.5	42	106.5
¾	20mm	or	2cm	9	23	26	66	43	109
⅞	22mm	or	2.2cm	10	25.5	27	68.5	44	112
1	25mm	or	2.5cm	11	28	28	71	45	114.5
1¼	32mm	or	3.2cm	12	30.5	29	73.5	46	117
1½	38mm	or	3.8cm	13	33	30	76	47	119.5
1¾	45mm	or	4.5cm	14	35.5	31	79	48	122
2	50mm	or	5cm	15	38	32	81.5	49	124.5
2½	65mm	or	6.5cm	16	40.5	33	84	50	127
3	75mm	or	7.5cm	17	43	34	86.5		
3½	90mm	or	9cm	18	46	35	89		
4	100mm	or	10cm	19	48.5	36	91.5		
4½	115mm	or	11.5cm	20	51	37	94		

YARDS TO METERS
(Slightly rounded off for convenience)

yards	meters	yards	meters	yards	meters	yards	meters	yards	meters
⅛	0.15	2⅛	1.95	4⅛	3.80	6⅛	5.60	8⅛	7.45
¼	0.25	2¼	2.10	4¼	3.90	6¼	5.75	8¼	7.55
⅜	0.35	2⅜	2.20	4⅜	4.00	6⅜	5.85	8⅜	7.70
½	0.50	2½	2.30	4½	4.15	6½	5.95	8½	7.80
⅝	0.60	2⅝	2.40	4⅝	4.25	6⅝	6.10	8⅝	7.90
¾	0.70	2¾	2.55	4¾	4.35	6¾	6.20	8¾	8.00
⅞	0.80	2⅞	2.65	4⅞	4.50	6⅞	6.30	8⅞	8.15
1	0.95	3	2.75	5	4.60	7	6.40	9	8.25
1⅛	1.05	3⅛	2.90	5⅛	4.70	7⅛	6.55	9⅛	8.35
1¼	1.15	3¼	3.00	5¼	4.80	7¼	6.65	9¼	8.50
1⅜	1.30	3⅜	3.10	5⅜	4.95	7⅜	6.75	9⅜	8.60
1½	1.40	3½	3.20	5½	5.05	7½	6.90	9½	8.70
1⅝	1.50	3⅝	3.35	5⅝	5.15	7⅝	7.00	9⅝	8.80
1¾	1.60	3¾	3.45	5¾	5.30	7¾	7.10	9¾	8.95
1⅞	1.75	3⅞	3.55	5⅞	5.40	7⅞	7.20	9⅞	9.05
2	1.85	4	3.70	6	5.50	8	7.35	10	9.15

AVAILABLE FABRIC WIDTHS

25"	65cm	50"	127cm
27"	70cm	54"/56"	140cm
35"/36"	90cm	58"/60"	150cm
39"	100cm	68"/70"	175cm
44"/45"	115cm	72"	180cm
48"	122cm		

AVAILABLE ZIPPER LENGTHS

4"	10cm	10"	25cm	22"	55cm
5"	12cm	12"	30cm	24"	60cm
6"	15cm	14"	35cm	26"	65cm
7"	18cm	16"	40cm	28"	70cm
8"	20cm	18"	45cm	30"	75cm
9"	22cm	20"	50cm		